Publication Manual

of the
American
Psychological
Association

Second Edition

Library of Congress Cataloging in Publication Data

American Psychological Association.
  Publication manual.

  First ed. published as v. 49, no. 4, pt. 2 (July 1952)
of Psychological bulletin.
  Bibliography: p.
  1. Communication in psychology. 2. Technical
writing. I. Title. DNLM: 1. Writing. WZ345 A518p
BF76.7.A46   1974   808'.02   74-11314
ISBN 0–912704–01–2

First printing, 1974
Second printing, 1975
Third printing, 1975
Fourth printing, 1976
Fifth printing, 1977

Copies may be ordered from:
Publication Sales
American Psychological Association
1200 Seventeenth Street, N.W.
Washington, D.C. 20036

Design by Brooke Todd & Associates, Arlington, Virginia
Composition by Hendricks-Miller Typographic Company, Washington, D.C.
Printing by Garamond/Pridemark Press, Inc., Baltimore, Maryland

Table of Contents

Foreword

Forty-six years ago, in 1928, editors and business managers of anthropological and psychological journals met to discuss the form of journal manuscripts and to write instructions for their preparation. The group agreed that it would not dictate to authors; instead, it recommended "a standard of procedure, to which exceptions would doubtless be necessary, but to which reference might be made in cases of doubt."

The outcome of that meeting was the forerunner of this book, published as a 7-page article in the February 1929 *Psychological Bulletin*. That first effort, sponsored by the National Research Council, was succeeded in 1944 by a 32-page guide authorized by the American Psychological Association's Board of Editors. This guide, which appeared in the *Psychological Bulletin* as an article by John Anderson and Willard Valentine, specifically stated that one of its aims was to encourage young members of the profession who might be writing for the first time.

In 1952 the renamed Council of Editors expanded the 1944 article into a 60-page supplement to the *Bulletin*. This revision marked the first appearance of the title *Publication Manual* and the beginning of a recognized APA journal style. Two revisions followed as separate publications, one in 1957 by the Council of Editors and another in 1967 by the APA Publications Office.

This 1974 edition of the Manual maintains the original intent of the early guides to help authors with the endless detail of manuscript preparation. However, this edition broadens that intent in several ways. It recognizes that what were once suggestions to authors of psychology articles are now course content for students of psychology. It also recognizes that, in 1929, APA could gently advise its authors on style because there were only 200 or so who reached print in the 4 APA journals. Today, the editors of APA's 14 journals consider more than 6,000 manuscripts a year with some 2,500 reaching print. Without APA style conventions, the cost in editing effort and time would be prohibitive, and clear communication would be jeopardized.

A final intent is less tangible. This edition of the Manual affirms the maturing of psychological language. It incorporates national and international standards of scientific communication and acknowledges other authorities on style. Although its style requirements are explicit, it recognizes alternatives to traditional forms and asks authors to balance the use of rules with good judgment. This Manual recognizes that changes in written language do not occur as fast as changes in the science itself; therefore, it does not prescribe for all stylistic problems. In that sense, it is a transitional document. It looks at the literature itself to determine forms rather than employing style to contain the literature.

The second edition has been prepared by members of the APA journal staff under the direction of Executive Editor Anita DeVivo. The project began with suggestions from many individuals, including psychology department chairmen, publishers, editors of APA and related journals, APA members, and technical editors in the APA Central Office. Susan Bunker of the journal staff coordinated the revision and wrote major portions of the manuscript. As members of a task force of the Publications and Communications Board, Charles Cofer, Robert Daniel, Frances Dunham, Walter Heimer, and William Mikulas wrote other portions of the manuscript. Mary Beyda of the journal staff was the technical editor and staff consultant on APA style.

As the principal advisory body, the APA Council of Editors has approved this Manual with enthusiasm. The Publications and Communications Board expresses its own endorsement of the second edition as a means to improving the quality of psychological communication.

The Publications and Communications Board
Arthur W. Melton, *Chairman*

Introduction

Rules for the preparation of manuscripts should contribute to clear communication. Take, for example, what some editors consider the most important rule: Double-space everything. A double-spaced manuscript allows each person in the publication process to function comfortably and efficiently: Authors and editors have space for handwritten notes; typists and printers can easily read all marks. Such mechanical rules, and most style rules, are usually arrived at by a consensus of established authorities and common usage. These rules introduce the uniformity necessary to convert manuscripts written in many styles to printed pages edited in one consistent style. They spare readers from a distracting variety of forms throughout a work, and permit them to give full attention to content.

This *Publication Manual* draws its rules from a large body of psychological literature, from editors and authors experienced in psychological writing, and from recognized authorities on publication practices. Writers who employ this Manual conscientiously will express their ideas in a form and style both accepted by and familiar to a broad readership in psychology.

In 1967, when the *Publication Manual* was revised, it was intended exclusively for APA authors. Since then, more students, more papers, and more journals have created an unprecedented need for common understandings in writing for psychology. In recognition of this need, the second edition is published for a more varied audience, including graduate and undergraduate students, editors, publishers, authors of non-APA journals, copy editors, typists, and printers.

For this wider readership, this edition expands the 1967 Manual, adds new sections, and reorganizes material in the sequence in which a manuscript is prepared. Thus, Chapter 1, Content and Organization of a Manuscript, discusses the purposes and nature of a journal article, how to conceptualize and structure ideas and data into elements of an article, and the author's responsibility for clear and accurate presentation of data.

Chapter 2, Writing Style, emphasizes the importance of making every word work toward the goal of clear and concise communication. It guides the researcher who, after gathering material, must write about it so it can be understood by readers.

Chapter 3, APA Editorial Style, deals with the seemingly endless details of grammar, punctuation, spelling, and references, those mechanical aspects of articles that cause debates among editors. This chapter does not duplicate other style books. Instead it resolves questions that occur most frequently in manuscripts written for psychological journals. It also recommends the forms that over the years have been accepted in APA journals and are now described as APA style.

Chapter 4, Typing, Mailing, and Proofreading, instructs authors and typists on preparing and assembling the final manuscript. A sample paper illustrates the variety of formats that can occur in one manuscript and demonstrates many applications of APA style.

Chapter 5 is about the American Psychological Association, its publication policies, and its journals. It explains the author's role in the production of journals and describes the procedures authors can expect after they submit their manuscripts.

The selected bibliography includes the references used to prepare this Manual, as well as a reading list. The appendixes contain a new section on preparing papers other than journal articles and a list of non-APA journals, also new.

Some features of this edition have been added for convenience to users. Examples appear in typewriter type. Material used frequently is easily accessible: Proofreader's marks appear inside the front cover; a checklist of common oversights in manuscript preparation appears inside the back cover; and a section illustrating a variety of reference citations appears at the back of the book. All material is cross-referenced, and a number system keyed to chapters should help readers locate material easily (number 4.17 indicates chapter 4, section 17). An expanded index uses these section numbers and is comprehensively cross-referenced.

Changes in requirements for manuscript preparation are inconvenient and annoying. They are, however, often unavoidable because of changes in printing technology, APA policy, progress in the science, or economic requirements. Should changes in requirements occur before the preparation of another Manual, they will be published in the *American Psychologist* and keyed to this edition. The announcements will be listed in the Journal's table of contents and in its annual volume contents.

Language lives in ideas. It cannot be fixed in a set of rules, a shelf of books, or an established science. This Manual does not concern itself with the everyday problems of writing and language so adequately dealt with elsewhere. Nor does it attempt to anticipate exceptional writing situations in psychology where style precedents may need to be set. When you find yourself without a rule or a reference and the answer to a question can be narrowed down to several reasonable and equally defensible choices, this Manual suggests that simplicity, plain language, and direct statements will always suffice.

Readers who are familiar with the previous edition should note the following changes introduced in this Manual. Decimal numbers in parentheses refer to sections in the Manual.

Policies
1. Authors may no longer request early publication. (5.2)
2. Authors are responsible for depositing any material for auxiliary publication. APA no longer performs this function. (Appendix A)

Manuscript Preparation
1. Some journals now require three copies of a manuscript. (Table 15)
2. Some journals now employ blind review procedures. (Table 15)

Manuscript Organization
1. Article title and by-line no longer carry footnote numbers. (3.64)
2. Authors now supply cover sheet and running head. (4.13)
3. An appendix is occasionally acceptable. (1.10)
4. Nonretrievable references cited in the manuscript are listed in a new "Reference Notes" section. (page 64)

Style
1. *Webster's New Collegiate Dictionary* (1973) is the authority for spelling and abbreviation. (3.74 and 3.3)
2. The abbreviations *S, E,* and *O* are no longer used in APA journals. (3.6)
3. Metric units are used. (3.8)
4. Statistical presentation used in the *Journal of Experimental Psychology* is now used in all journals. (3.14)
5. In displayed equations, equation numbers are enclosed in parentheses, not brackets. (3.17)
6. The letters (a), (b), and (c) in a series are not underlined. (4.16)
7. The source of a quotation is cited in parentheses, not brackets. (3.49)
8. Rules are to be used in tables only when necessary for clarity. (3.34)

References
1. References include only retrievable material. (page 60)
2. Arabic rather than roman numerals are used in reference lists. (3.59)
3. Volume numbers appear in italic rather than boldface type. (3.59)
4. The standard form of reference citation is simplified. (3.59)

1 Content and Organization of a Manuscript

PARTS OF A MANUSCRIPT

QUALITY OF CONTENT

1 Content and Organization of a Manuscript

A psychologist's research is complete when the results are shared with the scientific community. The traditional medium for communicating research results is scientific journals; therefore, the preparation of a manuscript for journal publication is an integral part of the research effort. This chapter considers how ideas and data are structured into an article.

Journal articles are usually *experimental reports, review articles,* or *theoretical articles.* The typical experimental report, essentially a formal research piece written for publication, consists of distinct sections that appear in a constant order: *Title, Author's Name* and *Institutional Affiliation, Abstract, Introduction, Method, Results, Discussion, References,* and occasionally an *Appendix.* Although the sections are distinct, their content is interrelated, so smooth transitions and integration of the parts of a paper are essential to a clear presentation of ideas.

Review articles, which survey particular areas of work in psychology, and theoretical articles, which advance or critically treat theoretical issues, require a different and more flexible organizational structure than experimental reports. Because the majority of journal articles are experimental reports, this discussion concentrates on their preparation.

Before writing an article, examine recent issues of appropriate journals for general orientation.

1.1 Length, Headings, and Tone

Three major characteristics of a journal article should be considered before writing begins: length, headings, and tone.

Length. Because of page limitations in APA journals, you should determine the typical length of an article in the journal for which you are writing and not exceed that length unless you are writing a monograph or other exceptional material. To calculate how long your manuscript might run in printed pages, divide the number of pages in your manuscript by 3 (i.e., 1 printed page = 3 manuscript pages).

Discursive writing tends to obscure an author's main points, and long manuscripts may frequently be improved by condensation. If a paper is too lengthy, it may be shortened by more precise writing, clear and direct statements, less discussion, deleting or combining tabular material, eliminating repetition, and writing in the active voice.

Headings. Carefully consider your material and the sequence and levels of importance of the ideas you wish to present. Headings are meant to help a reader grasp the outline of your paper and the relative importance of the parts of your paper (see pages 32–33).

Tone. Although scientific writing differs in form from literary writing, it need not and should not lack style or be dull. In describing your research, present the ideas and findings directly, but in an interesting and compelling manner that reflects your involvement with the problem (see chapter 2 on Writing Style).

Parts of a Manuscript

1.2
Title

The title should summarize the main idea of the paper simply and, if possible, with style. It should be a concise statement of the main topic and should refer to the major variables or theoretical issues you have investigated. It is frequently informative to state in the title the actual substantive variables under investigation, for example, "Reading Spatially Transformed Letters."

Because its principal function is to inform readers about the study, the title should be explanatory when standing alone. As a statement of article content, it is also used by indexers for publications such as *Psychological Abstracts* and other information retrieval systems. A good title easily compresses to the short title or running head used for editorial or printing purposes (see section 4.13).

Because a misleading title may be referenced inappropriately, avoid words that serve no useful purpose and only increase the length. For example, a reference to methods and results should not be included in the title, nor should the title begin with such redundancies as "A Study of" or "An Experimental Investigation of." To facilitate information retrieval, do not use abbreviations in the title. The recommended maximum length for the title is 12–15 words.

1.3
Author's Name and Institutional Affiliation

Every manuscript should have a by-line consisting of two parts: the name of the author and the institution at which the investigation occurred (without the words *by* or *from the*).

Author. The author's name should appear as it is customarily written; that is, an author should not use initials on one manuscript and full name on a later one. Omit titles (Dr. or Professor) and degrees (PhD, MD). Authorship should be limited to those who have made substantial scientific contributions to the study. If questions of authorship arise, consult Principle 17 (Publication Credit) of the APA "Ethical Standards of Psychologists" for guidelines. Assistants and colleagues who were not involved substantially in the work but who assisted in some way may be acknowledged in a footnote. Always obtain a person's consent before including his or her name in a footnote. (See section 3.63 on footnotes.)

Affiliation. If your institutional affiliation has changed since you completed your work, give your current affiliation in a footnote. Include a dual affiliation only if both institutions contributed financially to the study. List the department in the by-line only if it is other than a department of psychology. An author with no institutional connection should list his city and state below his name.

1.4 Abstract

An abstract is a brief summary of the content and purpose of the article. In APA journals the abstract is used in place of a concluding summary and appears directly under the by-line. All APA journals except *Contemporary Psychology* require an abstract.

The abstract allows readers to survey the contents of an article quickly. Because, like the title, it is used by *Psychological Abstracts* for indexing and information retrieval, the abstract should be self-contained and fully intelligible without reference to the body of the paper and suitable for publication by abstracting services without rewriting. Information or conclusions that do not appear in the main body of the paper should not appear in the abstract. Because so much information must be compressed into a small space, authors sometimes find the abstract difficult to write. Leaving it until the article is finished enables you to abstract or paraphrase your own words.

An abstract of a *research* paper should contain statements of the problem, method, results, and conclusions. Specify the subject population (number, type, age, sex, etc.) and describe the research design, test instruments, research apparatus, or data-gathering procedures as specifically as necessary to reflect their importance in the experiment. Include full test names and generic names of drugs used. Summarize the data or findings, including statistical significance levels, if any, as appropriate. Report inferences made or comparisons drawn from the results.

An abstract of a *review* or *theoretical* article should state the topics covered, the central thesis, the sources used (e.g., personal observation, published literature, or previous research bearing on the topic), and the conclusions drawn. It should be short but informative. For example, "The problem was further discussed in terms of Skinner's theory" is not an informative statement. The abstract should tell the reader the *nature* or *content* of the theoretical discussion: "The discussion of the problem centered on Skinner's theory and the apparent fallacy of determinism."

An abstract for a research paper should be 100–175 words; one for a review or theoretical article, 75–100 words. General style should be the same as that of the article.

Remember, to the degree that an abstract is succinct, accurate, quickly comprehended, and informative, it increases your audience.

1.5
Introduction

The main body of a paper opens with the introduction. Because the function of the introduction is obvious, it is not labeled. Its purpose is to inform the reader of the specific problem under study and the research strategy. In writing the introduction, consider: What is the point of the study? What is the rationale or logical link between the problem and the research design? What are the theoretical implications of the study and its relationship to previous work in the area? A good introduction answers these questions in a paragraph or two and gives the reader a firm sense of what you are doing and why.

In dealing with theory, clearly state the theoretical propositions tested and how they were derived. Summarize the relevant arguments and data and indicate how your experimental design and hypothesis relate to the issue.

Discuss the literature, but do not include an exhaustive historical review. Assume that the reader is a professional person generally familiar with the field and does not require a complete digest with each new paper. Cite only those selected studies pertinent to the specific issue; avoid references with tangential or general significance to the problem. In summarizing earlier works, avoid nonessential details; instead, emphasize major conclusions, findings, and relevant methodological issues. Refer the reader to general surveys or reviews of the topic if they are available.

Authors are obligated to acknowledge the contributions of others to the problem. Show the logical continuity between previous and present work. Develop the problem with enough breadth and clarity so it will be generally understood by as wide an audience as possible. Do not let the goal of brevity mislead you into writing a statement intelligible only to the specialist (and possibly not even to him or her).

Controversial issues, when relevant, should be treated fairly. A simple statement that certain studies support one conclusion while others support another conclusion is better than an extensive and inconclusive discussion. Whatever your personal opinion, avoid animosity and ad hominem arguments in developing the controversy. Do not attempt to support your position or to justify your research by citing established authorities out of context. Include only references that bear specifically on the problem at issue.

After you have introduced the problem and developed the background material, you are in a position to tell what you propose to do. This statement should be made in the closing paragraphs of the introduction. At this point, a definition of the variables and a formal statement of your hypotheses lend clarity to the article. Questions to bear in mind in closing the introduction are: What do I plan to manipulate? What results do I expect? Why do I expect them? The logic behind "Why do I expect them?" should be made explicit. The rationale for each hypothesis should be developed clearly.

1.6
Method

The method section should tell your reader how the study was conducted. The method should be described in enough detail to permit an experienced investigator to replicate the study if he or she so desires. A description also enables your reader to evaluate the appropriateness of your methods and the probable reliability of your results.

It is both conventional and convenient to divide the method section into labeled subsections. These will usually include, but not be limited to, a description of the *subjects,* the *apparatus* (or *materials*), and the *procedure.* If the design of the experiment is complex or the stimuli require detailed description, subheadings are warranted. These subheadings help readers to find specific information. Your own editorial judgment is probably the best guide on the question of the number and type of subheadings (see section 3.2 for guidelines).

A major question on these subsections is how much detail to include. Authors affect the quality of their manuscript by including too little or too much. The basic rule is: Include only information essential to comprehend and replicate the study. If you refer the reader elsewhere for details of the method, give a brief synopsis here.

Subjects. The subsection on subjects should answer three questions: Who participated in the study? How many participants were there? How were they selected? Give major demographic characteristics, such as sex and age, as well as any other relevant information. State the total number of participants and the number assigned to each experimental condition. If any participants did not complete the experiment, give the number and reasons. Report selection and assignment procedures, payments, promises made, general geographic location, and type of institutions utilized.

When animals are part of the study, report the genus, species, strain number, or other specific identification such as the name of the supplier. Give the number of animals used and their sex, age, and physiological condition. In addition, specify all details of their treatment and handling essential to the successful replication of the investigation.

When you submit your article, indicate to the journal editor that the treatment of participants (human or animal) was in accordance with the ethical standards of the APA (see APA *Ethical Principles in the Conduct of Research with Human Participants,* 1973, and *Principles for the Care and Use of Animals,* 1971).

Apparatus. The apparatus subsection should include a brief description of the apparatus or materials used and their function in the experiment. Standard laboratory equipment, such as furniture, stopwatches, or screens, can usually be mentioned without detail. Specialized equipment obtained from a commercial establishment should be identified by the firm's name and model number. In the case of complex or custom-made equipment, a drawing or photograph may be useful, although this adds to the printing cost.

Procedure. The procedure subsection should be a summary of each step in the execution of the research. It should include the instructions to the participants, the formation of the groups, and the specific experimental manipulations. Describe randomization, counterbalancing, and other control features in the design. State instructions in summary or paraphrase form, unless they are unusual or comprise an experimental manipulation, in which case they may be presented verbatim. Most readers are familiar with standard testing procedures; unless something new or unique is presented, do not describe the procedures in detail.

Remember that the method section should tell your reader *what* you did and *how* you did it.

Multiple experiments. When a series of experiments are reported, they are always labeled Experiment 1, Experiment 2, etc. These labels are main headings. They organize the subsections and make it convenient for the reader to refer to a specific experiment. With multiple experiments, the method and results sections of each experiment should appear under their appropriate experimental designation. A short discussion may also appear under each experimental heading (e.g., *Results and Discussion* combined), but a more inclusive, general discussion of all of the work should be included at the end of the article. Make the logic and rationale of each new experiment clear to your reader. For current practice in presenting multiple experiments, consult a recent issue of the journal you are writing for.

1.7 Results

The results should summarize the collected data and your statistical treatment of them. First, briefly state the main idea of your results or findings. Then, report the data in sufficient detail to justify your conclusions. Discussing the implications of the results is not appropriate here. Note all relevant results, including those that run counter to your hypotheses. Individual scores or raw data should not be included, although there are exceptions, such as single-subject designs or illustrative samples.

In reporting your data, choose the medium that presents them clearly and economically. It may be helpful to summarize your results and analysis in tables or figures, but do not repeat the same data in several places, and do not include tables with data that can be presented as well in a few sentences in the text. Use as few tables or figures as possible. Refer to all graphs, pictures, or drawings as "figures" and all tables as "tables." Figures and tables supplement the text; do not expect them to do the entire communication job. Always refer the reader to the figures and tables with sufficient explanation to make them readily intelligible (see sections 3.26–3.44 for detailed information on tables and figures).

Although figures are attractive and are useful in illustrating general trends, they are expensive to reproduce and imprecise when it comes to exact values. For these reasons, the tabular form for presenting data is preferable, especially for illustrating main effects. Of course, trends and interactions are best shown by figures.

In reporting tests of significance (t, r, χ^2, etc.), include information concerning the obtained magnitude or value of the test, the degrees of freedom, the probability level, and the direction of the effect (see sections 3.10–3.15 on statistical presentation). Assume that your reader has professional knowledge of statistics. Basic assumptions, such as rejecting the null hypothesis, should not be reviewed. However, if there is a question about the appropriateness of a particular test, be sure to justify its use.

Caution: Do not infer trends from data that fail by a small margin to meet the usual levels of significance. Such results are best interpreted as caused by chance and are best reported as such. Treat the results section like an income tax return: Take what's coming to you, but no more.

1.8 Discussion

After presenting the results, you are in a position to evaluate and interpret their implications, especially with respect to your original hypotheses. In the discussion section, you are free to examine, interpret, and qualify your results, as well as draw inferences from them. Give particular emphasis to any theoretical consequences of the results and the validity of your conclusions. (Where the discussion is relatively brief and straightforward, some authors prefer to combine it with the previous results section, yielding: *Results and Conclusions* or *Results and Discussion*.)

Open the discussion with a clear statement on the support or nonsupport of your original hypotheses. Similarities and differences between your results and the work of others should clarify and confirm your conclusions. Do not, however, simply reformulate and repeat points already made. Each new statement should contribute something to your position and to your readers' understanding of the problem. While certain shortcomings of the study may be noted and explained briefly, do not dwell compulsively on every flaw. Negative results should be accepted as such without an undue attempt to explain them away.

Avoid polemics and theoretical straw men in your discussion. Speculation is in order only if (a) it is identified as such, (b) it is related closely to empirical data or follows logically from theory, and (c) it is expressed concisely. If there are any practical implications to be drawn from your study, here is the place to mention them. Suggestions for improvements on your research or for new research are in order, but keep them brief.

In general, be guided by the following questions: What have I contributed here? How has my study helped to resolve the original problem? What conclusions and theoretical implications can I draw from my study? These questions are the core of your study, and readers have a right to clear, unambiguous, and direct answers.

1.9 References

Every article concludes with a list of all references cited in text. Just as data document interpretations and conclusions, reference citations document statements made about the literature. Choose references judiciously and cite them accurately. The standard procedures for citation are designed to help you provide accurate, complete references, useful to investigators and readers (see sections 3.51–3.62 and Appendix C).

1.10
Appendix

An appendix, although rarely used, is helpful under certain circumstances. If describing certain materials in depth would be distracting or inappropriate to the main body of the paper, you might include an appendix. Some examples of suitable material for an appendix are (a) a new computer program specifically designed for your research and unavailable elsewhere, (b) an unpublished test and its validation, (c) a complicated mathematical proof, or (d) a list of stimulus materials (e.g., those used in psycholinguistic research). The criterion for including an appendix should be whether it is useful to the reader in understanding, evaluating, or replicating your study. Material of either general or specialized interest should not be presented for its own sake.

Quality of Content

Now that you have prepared a manuscript, you may wish to submit it to a journal for review and for possible publication.

What are the possibilities of acceptance? For some time, rejection rates for the APA journals have been high. Approximately three out of four manuscripts are found unsuitable for publication. Of the successful manuscripts, few are acceptable as written; most require extensive revision. Although the reasons for rejection or revision may seem endless, some problems recur with sufficient frequency to warrant examination by authors, who often fail to consider the quality of their manuscripts from a journal editor's point of view. The discussion that follows considers some of the reasons an editor rejects a manuscript. It is taken from an editorial by Brendan A. Maher that appeared in the February 1974 *Journal of Consulting and Clinical Psychology.*

1.11
Piecemeal
Publication

Investigators engaged in systematic programs of research publish reports of their results from time to time as significant portions of their programs are completed. This practice is both legitimate and inevitable in research programs of several years' duration.

In contrast, editors sometimes receive papers in which a single investigation is broken into separate manuscripts submitted in a series. As a hypothetical example: A sample of subjects is administered a group of assessment techniques. Each assessment measure then provides the basis for a separate paper in which the introduction, literature survey, and description of method and subjects are more or less identical. The editor receives the separate papers only a few weeks apart. The author might have prepared one large report covering all of the data and thereby spared reviewers and readers duplication of effort and saved the journal badly needed space.

The same situation occurs when some subset of subjects receives additional treatment or measurement which is then reported in a new paper. Only when the editor examines the two papers jointly does it become evident that the sample of 50 in Paper 2 is a part of the sample of 100 in Paper 1, and that the various measures were administered at one sitting.

With such piecemeal reporting, journal editors usually defer decision on any item, returning all to the author with the suggestion that a single comprehensive paper would be more appropriate. APA journals publish monograph-length papers and thus are able to accommodate such integrated studies.

1.12 Single Correlations

Many manuscripts are reports of single correlational investigations. Thus, the correlation between the short and long form of a well-known assessment device will appear in a manuscript without reference to the validity or utility of either. Does the low correlation mean that the short form is a poor device? Or is it better than the long form? Is either form valid in any important clinical setting? Comparisons of two versions of a measure may be useful here, but these questions are not answered by simple correlational designs. Such reports may be methodologically sound but scientifically trivial. Editorial judgments of triviality are clearly more debatable than judgments that experiments lacking controls, for example, are useless. Nonetheless, with the aid of reviewers, they must be made.

1.13 Negative Results

Reports of negative results are a perennial and vexing problem. Reports of "no difference" between experimental groups or "no significance" in a correlation are of interest to editors under certain circumstances—for example, when an established theory clearly predicts that a difference or a correlation should be found. The investigator must make the theoretical deduction explicit and not leave it to "common sense" or "intuition." Negative results lacking a theoretical context are basically uninterpretable. Even when the theoretical basis for the prediction is clear and defensible, the burden of methodological precision falls heavily on the investigator who reports negative results. The greater the corpus of methodologically sound results supporting the theory, the heavier the burden.

Negative results are also valuable when an investigator discovers a methodological weakness in a published report of positive results and, correcting the weakness, finds that the significances vanish. Here it is less necessary that the theoretical significance of the results be articulated extensively if the prior report has attained some standing in the literature as a "finding."

Failure to replicate results of a previous investigator, using the same method but a different sample, is generally of questionable value. A single failure may merely testify to sampling error or to the conclusion that one of the two samples had unique characteristics responsible for the reported effect, or the lack of effect. An author can resolve the issue when he reports several failures with a range of samples. A single failure is too equivocal to justify publication on its merit alone.

<table>
<tr><td>

**1.14
Overspecific
Conclusions**

</td><td>

Research using the "bull in a Royal Worcester china shop" strategy sometimes is reported. To test the hypothesis that bulls have a desire to break Royal Worcester china, a shop is stocked exclusively with that item, the bulls are turned loose, and destruction ensues. The hypothesis is duly confirmed—especially if the control group is mice.

In a slightly disguised version of this same approach, a psychotic patient sample is compared with a control sample performing any task requiring motivation, attention, coordination, etc., and the conclusion is that the reason for the patients' deficiencies lies in some specific aspects of the particular task. Just as bulls tend to break any kind of china, patient populations tend to do poorly at many tasks. Thus, poor performance at a specific task is uninformative about the pathology unless it is accompanied by evidence of adequate performance at some other task that makes similar demands on general psychological functioning. A control task, or control response, is just as necessary as a control group when the hypothesis predicts poorer performance by one group.

</td></tr>
<tr><td>

**1.15
Faddism and
One-Shot Papers**

</td><td>

The field of psychology is occasionally marked by surges of enthusiasm for a new scale or technique. Publication begets publication until, inexplicably, enthusiasm wanes and the tidal wave subsides. Many manuscripts report single studies with the new scale on a specific population. Usually the author has not indicated why the scale should have significance for this population sample, a failing that could be corrected by elaborating on the relationship between the original theoretical foundation for the scale and the selection of the particular sample. The investigation appears to be a temporary enthusiasm rather than a systematic interest. Positive results devoid of theoretical explanation are only slightly less valuable than negative results in the same case.

Some problems that arise in manuscripts may be attributed to the publish-or-perish spirit in which they are written. Others, however, seem to arise because we become content with rapid, mediocre investigations where longer and more careful work is possible. The importance of the problems with which the APA journals are concerned is too great to make do with less reliable answers than it is possible to get. Authors, reviewers, and editors must work together to achieve the quality of information that readers deserve.

</td></tr>
</table>

2 Writing Style

2 Writing Style

Teaching the art of writing is beyond the scope of the *Publication Manual*. Instead, this chapter provides some general guidelines on effective writing, points out frequent faults, and suggests ways to assess and improve writing style. Mastery of grammar rules is not enough for good communication; craftsmanship in the use of language is also necessary. These guidelines are not intended to be so rigid that personal style is overly constrained, nor do they suggest the same style for all audiences.

To achieve clarity, good writing must be precise in its words, free of ambiguity, orderly in its presentation of ideas, economical in expression, smooth in flow, and considerate of its readers. A successful writer invites readers to read, encourages them to continue, and makes their task agreeable by leading them from thought to thought in a manner that evolves from clear thinking and logical development. The references in section 6.3 elaborate on these ideas.

2.1 Using the Precise Word

Make certain that every word used means exactly what it is intended to mean. Any writer, sooner or later, will discover that his own use of a word may not agree entirely with the definition in a standard dictionary. Prefixes are frequent troublemakers and require careful checking. For example, *disinterested* means impartial; *uninterested* means apathetic. Qualifiers are almost always a source of imprecision. Almost always? How much of the time is almost always? Expressions such as *quite a large part*, *practically all*, *very few*, and the like are interpreted differently by different readers or in different contexts. They weaken statements, especially those dealing with empirical observations.

Fortunately, choosing the precise word or phrase is easier for technical than for nontechnical concepts, where the choice is wider. The wider the choice, the greater the difficulty in selecting the exact word. Even the literate reader may be uncertain of the meaning of a rare or unfamiliar word.

Do not use words incorrectly (when you mean *think*, do not write *feel*); avoid colloquial expressions (use *insert*, not *put in*; *report*, not *write up*); and avoid coined terms (use *concept*, not *conceptuum*).

2.2 Avoiding Ambiguity

The referent for each term should be so apparent that the reader will not have to search over prior material. The simplest referents are the most troublesome: *which*, *this*, *that*, *these*, and *those*. If you include the referent every time you use *this*, *that*, *these*, and *those* (e.g., *this test* and *that trial*), you can avoid ambiguity. Avoid overuse of *this*, even with the referent. Also, make certain that the first sentence of a paragraph is comprehensible by itself; do not depend on a vague reference to earlier statements.

The editorial *we* is not used in scientific writing because it is often ambiguous. *We* means two or more authors or experimenters, including yourself. Use *I* when that is what you mean.

An awkward and often ambiguous construction results when a long string of modifiers is placed before the noun modified, especially when the modifiers are themselves nouns used as adjectives. For example, *a new performance test of motor skills used in colleges* is better than *a new motor skills performance college test*.

When writing about experimental groups, label them carefully. Using only numerals or letters can create ambiguity for the reader. Instead, whenever possible, use a key word to designate the treatment of each group. Remember that no reader is as familiar with your research as you are.

2.3 Orderly Presentation of Ideas

Thought units and sequences must be orderly. The reader expects continuity in words, concepts, and thematic development from opening statement to final conclusion, and is troubled by an author who misplaces words in sentences, abandons familiar syntax, shifts the criterion for items in a series, or clutters the sequence of ideas with irrelevancies. Reread the manuscript for coherence some time after the original writing and remove any barriers to an even progression.

Punctuation marks contribute to continuity by providing transitions between ideas. They cue the reader to the pauses, inflections, and pacing normally heard in speech, although punctuation differs in speech and writing. Some writers tend to overuse commas; others are too frugal with them. Overuse may annoy the reader; underuse can confuse him. Use punctuation to support meaning.

Although transitional words are sometimes used as a crutch, they can aid the reader attempting to follow a complex experimental design or an abstract theoretical development. Some transitional words are frequently misused. *While* does not mean *whereas* or *although*; *due to* and *since* do not mean *because*.

2.4 Economy of Expression

Short words are easier to comprehend than long words. However, the experienced writer will know when a long technical term should be selected for precision or when one long unusual word expresses an idea better than several short ones. The space necessary to express an idea lies somewhere between the terseness of telegraphic style and the circumlocution, excessive qualification, and verbiage of artificial scientific style. Authors in science are more often guilty of the

26

latter than the former. Wordiness, redundancy, evasiveness, and clumsiness characterize unprofessional writing.

By the same token, writing only in short, simple sentences produces choppy prose; but writing exclusively in long, involved sentences creates difficult if not unreadable material. Varying sentence length gives writing relief and interest. When involved concepts require long sentences, the components should march along like a parade, not dodge about like a broken-field runner.

The same cautions apply to paragraph length. Some writers construct paragraphs that are too long. On the other hand, many authorities on writing warn against short single-sentence paragraphs. Long material that does not break easily into paragraphs may need reorganization for clarity and logic. Even if reorganization is not necessary, consider breaking long paragraphs for visual relief.

2.5 Smoothness of Expression

Some linguistic situations can distract the reader: contradictions (real or inferred), insertion of the unexpected, omission of the expected, and sudden shifts. An author can usually catch real contradictions by reading a paper once for this fault alone. Inferred contradictions are more likely to surface if someone else reads the manuscript.

Do not introduce a topic abruptly. If the reader is likely to ask "How does that fit in?" more transition is necessary. This fault is common in literature reviews by graduate students, but it is not unknown among their mentors. Similarly, do not abandon an argument or development of a theme suddenly. If a reader feels "left hanging," the discussion needs a concluding statement.

Sudden shifts in tense should be avoided. Do not move capriciously between past and present tense within the same paragraph or successive paragraphs. Past tense is usually appropriate for a literature review (*Smith reported*) or the experimental design or procedure (*the judges were told*), inasmuch as it is a historical account. Use present tense to describe and discuss the results that are literally there before the reader (*shows auditory stimuli are more effective*). The present tense suggests a dialogue between author and reader, appropriate at that point of the paper. Future tense is rarely needed.

Obviously, verbs must agree with their subjects, and pronouns with the nouns to which they refer. This simple rule is usually not troublesome except with plural words of Latin or Greek origin that end in *a*. *Data*, *criteria*, and *phenomena* are plural, the high frequency of misuse notwithstanding. Check use of collective nouns; be certain that *faculty* or *staff*, for example, really refers to the collective group when using the singular verb or pronoun.

Frequently an author uses synonyms or near-synonyms to avoid repetition of a term. Although this intention is laudatory, the result may seriously detract from the flow of the paper. Learn to use a thesaurus, but with constraint. When a synonym is used, the reader cannot know if you intend to convey the *same* meaning as the first term or if a subtle difference in meaning is your intent. If monotony occurs, it may be from repeating ideas as well as words.

2.6 Consideration of the Reader

In scientific writing, devices that attract attention to words, sounds, or other embellishments, instead of ideas, are inappropriate. Heavy alliteration, accidental rhymes, poetic expressions, and clichés are suspect. They are unsuitable in scientific writing because they lead the reader, who is looking for information, away from the theme of the paper. Metaphors are sometimes helpful, but use them sparingly. Avoid mixed metaphors: Literal and figurative usages mix badly, to the detriment of communication; for example, "During the interview, the client sat with her head in her hands and her eyes on the floor."

Absolute insistence on the third person and the passive voice has been a strong tradition in scientific writing. Authorities on style and readability have clearly shown that this practice results in the deadliness and pomposity they call "scientificese." Some scientists maintain that this style preserves objectivity, but the validity of this assertion is suspect. Now, reputable journals are breaking the tradition with notable success, and writing manuals are recommending a more personal style. The *American National Standard for the Preparation of Scientific Papers* (1972) gives the following guideline:

> Authors should not always use verbs in the third person, passive voice. When a verb concerns the interaction of inanimate objects ("the membrane is acted upon by the drug"), the active voice is usually preferable ("the drug acts on the membrane") because it is more direct and concise. When a verb concerns an author's belief or conjecture, use of the impersonal passive ("it is thought" or "it is suggested") is highly inappropriate. When a verb concerns action by the author, he should use the first person, especially in matters of experimental design ("to eliminate this possibility, I did the following experiment"). Constant use of the first person is not advisable, however, since it may distract the reader from the subject of the paper. (p. 13)

An experienced writer can use the first person and the active voice without dominating the communication and without sacrificing the objectivity of the research. If any discipline should appreciate the value of personal communication, it should be psychology.

Finally, as a matter of consideration to readers, writers should be aware of the current move to avoid generic use of male nouns and pronouns when content refers to both sexes, and may wish to use alternatives to words such as *chairman* and to avoid overuse of the pronoun *he* when *she* or *they* is equally appropriate.

2.7 Criticism, Assistance, and Improvement

For many able researchers, writing is a difficult and irksome task, but writing, after all, is the expression of thinking. It is better to seek advice from others before submitting a manuscript than to hope that the editor will overlook faults. Choose a critic from outside your specialized research area. A spouse or close friend is usually not a good critic; enemies are better. If they do a good job, they may become friends. If material does not read well to an intelligent person who knows little of your area, it is probably presented poorly. Psychologists who communicate with only the dozen or so experts in their narrow specialties are not contributing significantly to the literature.

3 APA
Editorial Style

3   APA Editorial Style

When editors or printers refer to style, they usually do not mean writing style but editorial style, the rules or guidelines observed by a publisher to ensure consistency in the printed word. Editorial style is concerned with the uniform use of abbreviations, construction of tables, selection of headings, and citation of references, as well as many other elements that are part of every manuscript.

The author of a book may have considerable freedom in choosing his editorial style, but an author writing for a journal is subject to style rules established for that journal to avoid inconsistencies with other articles in the journal. For example, without style agreement, three different articles might use *sub-test*, *subtest*, and *Subtest* in one issue of a journal. Although the meaning is the same and the choice of one over the other may seem arbitrary (in this case, *subtest* is APA style), a defined editorial style produces uniform presentation and clear communication.

This chapter describes the editorial style for APA journals. It omits general rules covered in widely available style books and examples of usage with little relevance to APA journals. Among the most helpful general guides are the University of Chicago Press *Manual of Style* (1969), *Words into Type* (Skillin & Gay, 1974), and the U.S. Government Printing Office *Style Manual* (1973), all used in developing this section. These style books agree more often than they disagree; where they disagree, this Manual, because it considers the special requirements of psychology, takes precedence for the APA journals.

Headings

Headings indicate the organization of an article and establish the importance of each topic. Topics of equal importance are positioned consistently in the manuscript. (See section 4.16 for detailed typing instructions.)

3.1
Levels of
Headings

Most articles in APA journals use two or three levels of headings, which are positioned in this way:

A Centered Main Heading

A Flush Side Heading

    An indented paragraph heading.

The three headings would look like this in a manuscript:

Method

Procedure

    Pretraining period.

3.2
Guidelines for
Headings

All levels of headings are not appropriate in every article. Use the following guidelines for determining the level and position of headings:

- *One* level of heading may be sufficient for a short article. In such cases, use only centered main headings.

- *Two* levels of headings meet the requirements of most articles. Use centered main headings as the principal headings, with flush side headings for the second level. However, when the subordinate material is short, or when a great number of second headings are necessary, indented paragraph headings may be more appropriate for the second level.

- When *three* levels of headings are required, use centered main headings, followed by flush side headings and indented paragraph headings.

- If the article requires *four* levels of headings, subordinate the three levels above by introducing another centered heading in all capital letters.

EXPERIMENT 1

Method

Procedure

    Pretraining period.

Use four levels of headings only when content is detailed enough; four are most appropriate for articles reporting a series of related experiments, monographs, and lengthy literature reviews.

- Do not use a heading for the introduction.

- Do not number or letter headings. The varying styles of headings and their arrangement should reveal the organization sufficiently. (The numbering of sections in the Manual is an exception in order to permit indexing and cross-referencing.)

Abbreviations

3.3
Use of
Abbreviations

APA journals use abbreviations sparingly. APA journal style recognizes that abbreviations are sometimes useful for long, technical terms in scientific writing, but more may be lost than gained by their use, especially if the abbreviation is unfamiliar to the reader. Consider whether the space saved by abbreviations in the following passage justifies the time necessary to master the meaning:

```
The advantage of the LH was clear from the RT data,
which reflected high FP and FN rates for the RH.
```

Without abbreviations the passage reads:

```
The advantage of the left hand was clear from the
reaction time data, which reflected high false pos-
itive and false negative rates for the right hand.
```

In the following example, however, a standard abbreviation for a long familiar term eases the reader's task:

```
The MMPI was administered to patients at seven
hospitals.
```

On the principle that excessive use of abbreviations, whether standard or explained, can hinder reading comprehension, in 1969 the APA Council of Editors and the Publications Board acted to eliminate from APA journal articles all idiosyncratic abbreviations (those specific to the article itself). For standardization, authors were requested to use only those abbreviations in S. J. Reisman's book *A Style Manual for Technical Writers and Editors* (now out of print). Reisman provided these helpful guidelines on the use of abbreviations: (a) if the reader is more familiar with the abbreviation than with the complete form; (b) if the use of an abbreviation is conventional; or (c) if considerable space can be saved and cumbersome repetition avoided.

Preserving the intent of the policy within Reisman's guidelines, APA style permits the following use of abbreviations:

- Use abbreviations that appear as word entries (i.e., are not labeled *abbr*) in *Webster's New Collegiate Dictionary* (1973). Examples:

```
IQ   LSD   REM   ESP
```

Such abbreviations may be used without further explanation.

- Use abbreviations that are not in the dictionary but appear frequently in the journal for which you are writing. Authors should note that these abbreviations, although probably well understood by many readers, must always be explained when first used (see section 3.4). Examples:

MMPI   CS   CA   ITI   CVC   STM   RT

- Use abbreviations for standard Latin terms, statistics, and reference terms, as described in sections 3.7, 3.12, and 3.59, respectively.

- Use abbreviations for metric units. When writing for the *Journal of Experimental Psychology* and the *Journal of Comparative and Physiological Psychology*, abbreviate nonmetric units as well. (See sections 3.8 and 3.9 for further discussion on metric units.)

Under all other circumstances, the writer must decide (a) whether to spell out a given expression every time it is used in an article or (b) whether to spell it out initially and abbreviate it thereafter. For example, the abbreviations L for large and S for small in a paper discussing different sequences of reward (LLSS or LSLS) would be an effective and readily understood shortcut. In another paper, it would be both unnecessary and confusing to talk about the L reward and the S reward. Another example is the use of abbreviations for group names. It is better not to use abbreviations for this purpose, but if absolutely necessary, make the abbreviated names as meaningful as possible. In general, consider your readers and use only those abbreviations that will help you to communicate with them.

**3.4
Explanation of
Abbreviations**

Because the acronyms that psychologists employ in their daily writing may not be familiar to students or readers in other disciplines or other countries, acronyms and abbreviations should be explained.

A term to be abbreviated must, on its first appearance, be spelled out completely and immediately followed by its abbreviation in parentheses. Thereafter, the abbreviation is used.

Studies of simple reaction time (RT) to a visual target have found a strong negative relationship between RT and luminance.

**3.5
Use of Periods
with
Abbreviations**

Use the following guide for the use of periods with abbreviations.

Use periods with:

- initials of names (J. R. Smith)
- abbreviations of state and territory names (N.Y.; Washington, D.C.; U.S. Navy)
- Latin abbreviations (i.e.; vs.; a.m.)
- reference abbreviations (Vol. 1; 2nd ed.; p. 6)
- nonmetric measurement abbreviations where used (ft.; lb.)

Do not use periods with:

- capital letter abbreviations and acronyms (APA; DNA; UNESCO; IQ; PhD)
- metric measurement abbreviations (cm; kg; cd)

3.6 Subject, Experimenter, and Observer

The abbreviations *S, E,* and *O* for subject, experimenter, and observer are no longer used in APA journals. If a generic term, such as *patients, children,* or *rats,* better describes the experimental group, use that term rather than *subjects.*

3.7 Standard Latin Abbreviations

The following Latin abbreviations are usually used in parenthetical material:

cf.	compare to	i.e.,	that is
et al.	and others	viz.,	namely
etc.	and so forth	vs.	versus, against
e.g.,	for example		

Metrication

3.8 Policy on Metrication

At their 1969 spring meetings, the APA Council of Editors and the Publications Board voted to adopt the metric system in all APA journals and to require that all references to physical measurements, where feasible, follow the metric system. The APA adopted the International System of Units (SI), an extension and refinement of the traditional metric system. SI is the system adopted by the General Conference of Weights and Measures in 1960 and recommended by the national standardizing bodies in many countries, including the United States.

The transition to SI is a long and complex task, and at this writing, the move toward the exclusive use of metric units in the United States is gradual. In preparing manuscripts, authors should use metric units if possible; however, during the transition, many experimenters will have to use instruments that record measurements in nonmetric units until new instruments are available. Measurements expressed in nonmetric units are acceptable in APA journals *if accompanied by established SI equivalents in parentheses:*

The rods were spaced 19 mm apart.
[Measurement was made in metric units.]

The rod was 3 ft. (.91 m) in length.
[Measurement was made in nonmetric units and converted to SI equivalents.]

Journal editors reserve the right to return manuscripts if measurements are not expressed properly.

The following tables are intended to assist authors in the conversion to metrication. For more detailed information, consult the references on metrication listed in section 6.3.

Table 1: SI Base Units

Quantity	Name	Symbol
length	meter	m
mass	kilogram	kg
time	second	sec
electric current	ampere	A
thermodynamic temperature[a]	kelvin	K
amount of substance	mole	mol
luminous intensity	candela	cd

[a] Celsius temperature is generally expressed in degrees Celsius (symbol °C).

Table 2: SI Derived Units

Quantity	Name	Symbol
area	square meter	m^2
volume	cubic meter	m^3
speed, velocity	meter per second	m/sec
acceleration	meter per second squared	m/sec^2
wave number	1 per meter	m^{-1}
density, mass density	kilogram per cubic meter	kg/m^3
concentration (of amount of substance)	mole per cubic meter	mol/m^3
activity (radioactive)	1 per second	sec^{-1}
specific volume	cubic meter per kilogram	m^3/kg
luminance	candela per square meter	cd/m^2

Table 3: SI Derived Units with Special Names

Quantity	Name	Symbol	Expression in terms of other units
frequency	hertz	Hz	
force	newton	N	
pressure	pascal	Pa	N/m^2
energy, work, quantity of heat	joule	J	N·m
power, radiant flux	watt	W	J/sec
quantity of electricity, electric charge	coulomb	C	A·sec
electric potential, potential difference, electromotive force	volt	V	W/A
capacitance	farad	F	C/V
electric resistance	ohm	Ω	V/A
conductance	siemens	S	A/V
magnetic flux	weber	Wb	V·sec
magnetic flux density	tesla	T	Wb/m^2
inductance	henry	H	Wb/A
luminous flux	lumen	lm	
illuminance	lux	lx	

Table 4: SI Supplementary and Derived Units

Quantity	Name	Symbol
plane angle	radian	rad
solid angle	steradian	sr
angular velocity	radian per second	rad/sec
angular acceleration	radian per second squared	rad/sec^2
radiant intensity	watt per steradian	W/sr
radiance	watt per square meter steradian	W·m^{-2}·sr^{-1}

Table 5: SI Prefixes

Factor	Prefix	Factor	Prefix
10^{12}	tera	10^{-1}	deci
10^9	giga	10^{-2}	centi
10^6	mega	10^{-3}	milli
10^3	kilo	10^{-6}	micro
10^2	hecto	10^{-9}	nano
10^1	deca	10^{-12}	pico

Table 6: Examples of Conversions to SI Equivalents

Physical quantity	Traditional unit	SI equivalent
length	inch	.0254 m
	micron	10^{-6} m
	angstrom	10^{-10} m
area	square inch	645.16 mm^2
volume	cubic inch	16.3871 cm^3
capacity	fluid ounce	29.5737 cm^3
mass	grain	64.7989 mg
	ounce	28.3495 g
	U.S. pound	.4536 kg
illumination	footcandle	10.7639 lx
luminance	footlambert	3.42626 cd/m^2
	millilambert	3.1827 cd/m^2
energy	calorie (IT)	4.1868 J
force	dyne	10^{-5} N
pressure [a]	pound/square inch	6894.76 N/m^2
	10 dynes/cm^2	1 N/m^2

[a] The common reference for sound pressure level (SPL) is the audibility threshold at 1,000 Hz or 20 μN/m^2. The traditional unit of SPL was .0002 dynes/cm^2. Decibel (db.) is a ratio and is meaningless unless one term of the ratio is given, for example, 70 db. re 20 μN/m^2.

Statistics

To present statistical data in a clear and interesting way within the space limits of a journal article is a challenge. Most writers use some combination of textual presentation, tables, and figures. By observing the following conventions, you can help your reader to understand the data.

3.10
Reference
Citation

Do not give a reference for statistics in common use; this convention applies to the majority of statistics used in journal articles. Do give a reference for (a) less commonly used statistics, especially those that have appeared in journals but are not yet incorporated in textbooks; or (b) a controversial use of a statistic (e.g., justification for a test of significance when the data do not meet the assumptions of the test). When the statistic itself is the focus of the article, give supporting references (see sections 3.51–3.62).

3.11
Formulas

When deciding whether to include formulas, follow the intent of the citation rules above. That is, do not give a formula for common statistics; do give a formula for a statistic not yet widely known or for one that is itself the focus of the article. Presentation of the equation in the text is described in sections 3.16–3.19.

3.12
Italics

With the exception of Greek letters, underline all letters used as statistical symbols. They are italicized in print wherever they appear (text, tables, and figures). However, subscripts and superscripts usually are not italicized.

M	F	n	SS_b
SD	t	N	SS_w
Mdn	df	r	MS
z	p	R	MS_e

3.13
Greek Letters
as Statistical
Symbols

Population (as opposed to sample) values are indicated by Greek letters. In addition, a few sample statistics (such as χ^2 and some correlation coefficients) are expressed by Greek letters, which usually need to be written in by hand. To avoid any possibility of misunderstanding a Greek letter, write out the name of the letter above it.

(mu) (beta) (tau) (sigma)
μ β τ Σ

3.14
Textual
Presentation

To present a statistic in text, give name, degrees of freedom, value, and probability level. Use the following form, adopted by all APA journals:

As predicted, the first-grade girls reported a significantly greater liking for school than did the first-grade boys, $\underline{t}$ (22) = 2.62, $\underline{p}$ < .01.

The analysis of variance indicated a significant retention interval effect, $\underline{F}$ (1, 34) = 123.07, $\underline{p}$ < .001.

When enumerating a series of similar statistics, be certain that the relationship between the statistics and their referents is clear. Words such as *respectively* and *in order* can clarify this relationship:

Means for Trials 1 through 4 were 2.43, 2.59, 2.68, and 2.86, respectively.

In order, means for Trials 1 through 4 were 2.43, 2.59, 2.68, and 2.86.

When using a statistical term in the narrative, use the term, not the symbol. For example, use "The means were," not "The *M*s were."

3.15
Tabular
Presentation

If the experiment has a complex design with many *F* ratios, tabular presentation is clearer and more efficient. Submit appropriate analysis of variance tables with the manuscript for publication at the editor's discretion.

Mathematical Copy

Because typesetting mathematical material is a difficult and expensive process, do not include extensive mathematical or statistical formulas unless they are new, rare, or essential to the paper. When mathematical copy is included, the time and cost of typesetting can be reduced if manuscripts are prepared according to the directions in this section. For more detailed information, consult the references on mathematical copy in section 6.3.

3.16
Equations
in Text

- Place short and simple equations, such as $a = [1 + b)/x]^{1/2}$, in the line of text.

- Equations in the line of text should not project above or below the line; for example, the equation above would be difficult to set if

  it were in the form $a = \sqrt{\dfrac{1 + b}{x}}$.

- To present fractions in one line in text, use a slanted line (/) and appropriate parentheses and brackets.

    a. Use ( ) first, then [( )], and finally { [( )] } .

    b. Use parentheses and brackets to avoid ambiguity: Does $a/b + c$ mean $(a/b) + c$ or $a/(b + c)$?

3.17 Displayed Equations

- Simple equations should be displayed (set off from text) if they must be numbered for later reference.

- Display all complex equations on a widely spaced line.

- Number displayed equations consecutively, with the number in parentheses near the right margin of the page:

$$\chi = -2 \sum a_x{}^2 + a_0 + \frac{\cos x - 5ab}{1/n + a_x} \tag{1}$$

- When referring to numbered equations, spell out Equation 1 (not Eq. 1) or say "the first equation."

3.18 Marking Letters and Symbols

- Some letters, numerals, and other characters may be ambiguous to the printer (see Equation 1 in section 3.17). In typewritten and handwritten copy, ambiguity may occur in the following: 1 (one or the letter el), 0 (zero or the letter oh), X (multiplication sign or the letter ex), Greek letters (B or beta), and some handwritten capital and lowercase letters (e.g., **c, s,** and **x**). When they first appear in the manuscript, identify ambiguous and handwritten characters with penciled notations (e.g., "lowercase el throughout"). If many such characters or special symbols occur in a paper, submit a list of the characters or symbols for the printer. If possible, avoid symbols or letters with marks directly above or below the letter because they must be set by hand (e.g., use a' not $á$).

- In addition to identifying symbols, underline all letters that represent mathematical variables; these will be set in *italic* type. Do not underline Greek letters or any abbreviation that is not a variable (e.g., sin, log). Mark vectors with wavy underlining (V); these will be set in **boldface** type (but vector components are set in *italic* type).

- Use the symbol for percent (%) only when preceded by a number. Use the word *percentage* when a number is not given.

  found that 18% of the rats

  determined the percentage of rats

- Space mathematical copy as you would space words: $a+b=c$ is as difficult to read as wordswithoutspacing; $a + b = c$ is much better.

- Align mathematical copy carefully. Subscripts usually precede superscripts $(x_a{}^2)$, but a prime is set next to a letter or symbol (x'_a). If an equation exceeds the column width of a journal, the printer will decide how to break it.

- Punctuate all equations, whether they are in the line of text or displayed, to conform to their place in the syntax of the sentence (see Equation 1 in section 3.17).

  In general, remember that the copy editor and the printer, who will convert the manuscript to a printed version, usually do not have mathematical backgrounds and will reproduce what they see, not what a mathematician knows. Avoid misunderstandings and expensive errors by carefully preparing mathematical copy.

Numbers

Some numbers are expressed in words according to general usage and the need for typographic solidity.

Use words to express:

- the numbers zero through nine

  A total of five lists of 32 words each were presented to the children.

  The subjects were six undergraduates.

  The cage contained two levers.

  Exceptions: See section 3.21.

- any number, above or below 10, that begins a sentence

  Sixty-four items were on the list.

  One hundred and six undergraduates served as subjects.

  Six percent of the total responses were errors.

  Note: If possible, rewrite a sentence to avoid starting with a number.

Numbers of two or more digits and numbers in technical, scientific, or statistical matter are easier to comprehend when they are expressed in figures. Use the following guidelines to determine appropriate forms for numbers:

Use figures to express:

- numbers 10 or greater

    a total of 64 lists

- any numbers, above or below 10, that are:

units of measurement or time, abbreviated or not	were given 5-mg drug pellets daily for 3 days
ages	was 6 years old
times and dates	8:30 a.m. on May 6, 1972
percentages	a total of 6%
arithmetical manipulation	multiplied by 3
ratios	4:1
fractional or decimal quantities	a 2½-year-old 2.54 cm
exact sums of money	were paid $5 each
scores and points on a scale	was 4 on a 7-point scale
actual numerals	the numerals 1–6
page numbers	on page 2
series of four or more	1, 3, 5, and 7
numbers grouped for comparison within a sentence or a series of related sentences if any one of the numbers is 10 or more. (Let clarity be the guide in applying this rule.)	Of the 40 trials, 6 were practice trials. Included in the 14-pair list were 7 nouns, each occurring in 2 pairs, and 14 adjectives, each occurring in 1 pair.

If figures and words appear together, try recasting the sentence:

The group had 48 men and 38 women.

   is better than

Forty-eight men and 38 women were in the group.

**3.22
Ordinal
Numbers**

Treat ordinal numbers as you would cardinal numbers (see sections 3.20 and 3.21).

the fifth list for the first-grade students
the 75th trial (or Trial 75)

Exception: Percentiles and quartiles are always figures.

5th percentile   1st quartile

3.23
Arabic
or Roman
Numerals

Because roman numerals are cumbersome and difficult to read, use arabic numerals wherever possible.

Experiment 1   Group 3   Vol. 3

Exception: If roman numerals are part of an established terminology, do not change to arabic numerals.

Type II error   Factor I

3.24
Commas
in Numbers

In most figures of 1,000 or more, use commas between every group of three digits in text and in tables.

1,536 items   34,587 pellets

3.25
Decimal
Fractions

A zero is not used before the decimal point in decimal numbers less than one.

$\underline{p} < .05$ $\underline{r} = +.82$

Use decimal fractions instead of mixed fractions (6.25, not 6¼) unless mixed fractions are more appropriate (e.g., a 2½-year-old).

Tables

3.26
Tabular
Versus
Textual
Presentation

Tables are complicated to set in type and, therefore, are more expensive to publish than straight text. For this reason, they are best reserved for important data directly related to the content. However, a well-constructed table can be economical in that it compresses data and allows the reader to see relationships not readily discernible in text. Compare the following presentations:

The mean numbers of words reported for the three subjects were 2.6, 2.8, and 1.6 at the 25-msec interstimulus interval; 3.0, 1.8, and 2.2 at the 50-msec interstimulus interval; 2.6, 2.0, and 2.8 at the 75-msec interstimulus interval; and 3.0, 3.0, and 3.0 at the 100-msec interstimulus interval.

Table 7
Mean Number of Words Reported as a
Function of Interstimulus Interval

	Interstimulus interval (in msec)			
Subject	25	50	75	100
1	2.6	3.0	2.6	3.0
2	2.8	1.8	2.0	3.0
3	1.6	2.2	2.8	3.0

The reader can more easily comprehend and compare the data presented in tabular form.

Determine the amount of data necessary for the reader to understand the discussion and then decide whether those data are best presented in text or tabular form. Peripherally related or extremely detailed data should be omitted or, depending on their nature, deposited in a national retrieval center (see Appendix A, NAPS).

3.27
Relationship
Between
Tables and Text

A good table supplements, not duplicates, the text. In the text, refer to every table and its data. However, discuss only the highlights in the text; if every item is discussed, the table becomes unnecessary.

In addition to being integrated into the text, each table should be intelligible without reference to the text. Use a descriptive title as well as notes or subheadings to explain abbreviations, italics, parentheses, and units of measurement (see Table 8). In the text, refer to tables by their numbers:

as shown in Table 8, the responses

children with pretraining (see Table 8).

Avoid such references as "the table above/below" or "the table on page 32" because the position and page number of a table cannot be determined until the pages are made up by the printer. However, indicate to the printer the approximate placement of each table in the text (see section 4.20 for instructions).

Table 8

Mean Number of Correct Responses on Verbal Tests
by Children With and Without Pretraining

Title explains group names

Group	n [a]	Grade 3	Grade 6
Girls			
With	20 (18)	280	319
Without	20 (19)	240	263
Boys			
With	20 (19)	281	317
Without	20 (20)	232	262

Note to table gives total score for comparison with entries in table.

Note. Maximum score = 320.

Footnote to n column explains use of parentheses.

[a] Numbers in parentheses indicate the number of children who completed all tests.

44

3.28
Relationship Between Tables

Ordinarily, an identical column of figures should not appear in two tables. When two tables overlap, consider combining them.

To facilitate comparison among tables in a paper, be consistent in the presentation of all tables. For example, use the same terminology (*response time* or *reaction time*, but not both) and similar forms for titles and headings.

3.29
Table Numbers

Number all tables with arabic numerals in the order in which they are first mentioned in text. Do not use suffix letters to indicate relationships between tables; that is, do not refer to Tables 5, 5A, and 5B, but to Tables 5, 6, and 7, or combine the related tables. If the manuscript includes an appendix with tables, identify them with capital letters (e.g., Table A).

3.30
Table Titles

Give every table a brief but clearly explanatory title. Use a telegraphic style to identify the table.

too telegraphic: Relationship Between College
Majors and Performance

(unclear as to what data are presented in table)

too detailed: Mean Performance Scores on Test A,
Test B, and Test C of Students
with Psychology, Physics, English,
and Engineering Majors

(duplicates information in the headings of the table)

good title: Mean Performance Scores of
Students with Different College
Majors

3.31
Column Headings

A table compares or classifies related items. Data form the body of the table. Correct headings can establish the logic of the body and organize it efficiently. Depending on the complexity of the table, headings may be stubheads, boxheads, column heads, or spanner heads (see Table 9 in this section).

The left-hand column (called a *stub*) usually lists the major independent variables. This column always has a heading (the *stubhead*), which describes the elements listed in that column (the *stub column*). In Table 7, the stub lists the subjects; in Table 8, the groups.

Subordination within the stub column is better indicated by indention of stub items than by creation of an additional column (see Tables 8 and 9):

Poor:	Sex	Pretraining	Better:	Group
	Girls	With		Girls
		Without		With
	Boys	With		Without
		Without		Boys
				With
				Without

The headings at the top of the table (called *boxheads*) identify the entries in the vertical columns in the body of the table. A boxhead may cover just one column (see Table 8), or it may be subdivided to cover several columns which carry column heads (see Table 7). Often a boxhead can be used to avoid repetition of words in column headings (see Table 9):

Poor:	Grade 3	Grade 4	Grade 5	Grade 6
Better:	Grade			
	3	4	5	6

A few tables may require spanner headings in the body of the table. These headings span the entire width, allowing for further divisions within the table (see Table 9). Also, spanners can be used to combine two tables into one.

Any item within a column should be syntactically as well as conceptually comparable to the other items in that column, and all items should be described by the heading:

Poor:	Trait	Better:	Trait
	Intelligent		Intelligent
	Aggression		Aggressive
	Talks a lot		Talkative

**3.32
Body
of the
Table**

The body of the table contains the numerical data. Express the values only to the number of significant figures that the accuracy of the measurements justifies. It is important not to change the unit of measure in a column.

Table 9

Mean Number of Correct Responses by Children

With and Without Pretraining

Group	$\underline{n}$[a]	Grade			
		3	4	5	6
Verbal tests					
Girls					
With	20 (18)	280	297	301	319
Without	20 (19)	240	251	260	263
Boys					
With	20 (19)	281	290	306	317
Without	20 (20)	232	264	221	262
Mathematical tests					
Girls					
With	20 (20)	201	214	221	237
Without	20 (17)	189	194	216	135[b]
Boys					
With	20 (19)	210	236	239	250
Without	20 (18)	199	210	213	224

Note. Maximum score = 320.

[a] Numbers in parentheses indicate the number of children who completed all tests.

[b] One girl in this group made only 2 correct responses.

(Handwritten annotations: "stubhead" points to Group; "stub column" points to the Girls/Boys column; "boxhead" points to Grade; "column head" points to 3 4 5 6; "spanner headings" point to Verbal tests and Mathematical tests.)

Do not include columns of data that can be calculated easily from other columns:

Poor:

Subject	No. solved	% solved
1	11	68.75
2	8	50.00
3	15	93.75

Note. Each subject had 16 problems to solve.

Better:

Give either the number or the percentage data, whichever is important to the discussion.

3.33
Footnotes
to a
Table

Footnotes to a table have three functions:

- A *general* note qualifies, explains, or provides information relating to the table as a whole.

- A *specific* note refers to a particular column or individual entry.

- A *probability level* note indicates the results of tests of significance.

Each note takes a different form:

- A *general* note is designated by the word *Note* followed by a period. (See also section 3.36 for an example of a general note indicating that the table is reprinted from another source.)

  Note. Columns total more than 100% because respondents could mark more than one response.

- A *specific* note is indicated by superscript lowercase letters ([a], [b], [c]). Order the superscripts horizontally across the table by rows. Specific notes to a table are independent of any other table and begin with [a] in each table. (See Tables 8 and 9 for examples of this kind of note.)

- Asterisks indicate the *probability levels* of tests of significance. When more than one level is used in a table, use one asterisk for the lowest level and progress upward. Probability levels and number of asterisks need not be consistent among tables.

F
2.80*
1.66
4.38**

*$\underline{p}$ < .05.

**$\underline{p}$ < .01.

Order the footnotes to a table in the following manner:

<u>Note</u>. The subjects . . .

$^{a}\underline{n} = 25.$

$^{b}\underline{n} = 42.$

$^{*}\underline{p} < .05.$

$^{**}\underline{p} < .01.$

Certain types of information may be appropriate either in the table or in a footnote. To determine placement of such material, remember that the objective of the table is to present a quantity of related material clearly in the least space. Thus, if *ps* or *ns* are numerous, use a column rather than many notes. Conversely, if a row or column contains few entries (or the same entry), eliminate the column by adding a footnote to the table:

Poor:	Group	$\underline{n}$	Better:	Group[a]
	1	15		1
	2	15		2
	3	15		3

$^{a}\underline{n} = 15$ for each group.

3.34 Ruling of Tables

When tables are set in type, they may have (a) no rules, (b) either vertical or horizontal rules, or (c) both vertical and horizontal rules. Some APA journals rule tables both vertically and horizontally, but printing requirements are leading to a more selective use of rules, with clarity in print the determinant.

In the typewritten manuscript, use generous spacing between columns and rows and proper alignment to clarify relationships within a table. When rules are used, draw them in pencil so that they may be changed if necessary for printing requirements. (See section 4.20 for detailed typing instructions.)

3.35 Size of Tables

Turning a journal sideways to read a table is an inconvenience to readers. A table can be designed to fit a journal page or column by counting characters (i.e., letters, numbers, and spaces). Count characters in the widest entry in each column (body or headings) and allow three characters for spaces between columns. If the count exceeds 100, the table will not fit across most APA journal *pages*. If it exceeds 50, it will not fit across most APA journal *columns*. To determine exact fit, count the characters in the journal for which you are writing and adjust your table if necessary.

3.36
Tables
from
Another
Source

An author must obtain permission to reproduce an entire table from a copyrighted source. Enclose the letter of permission when submitting the manuscript. Also, include a note at the bottom of the reprinted table giving credit to the original author and copyright holder. The note takes the following form:

Note. From "Title of Article" by A. N. Author and C. O. Author, Title of Journal, 1966, 50, 22-32. Copyright 1966 by the Name of Copyright Holder. Reprinted by permission.

The same form is used for reprinted text or figures. If only selected data or parts of a table are derived from another work, simply acknowledge the source (e.g., "The data in column 1 are from Author and Author, 1966"). If there is any doubt about the policy of the copyright holder, permission should be requested.

Figures, Graphs, and Illustrations

Illustrative materials, such as figures, charts, graphs, and photographs, often increase understanding of the text in a way that lengthy discussion cannot. Because the design and preparation of such material can be expensive to both authors and publishers, use illustrations judiciously. Ask yourself whether the illustration is necessary: Does it extend or clarify the discussion? Does it supplant text? Does it simply repeat text? Illustrations and text should complement, rather than repeat, each other. In this discussion, all illustrative material is called figures.

Preparation for printing varies with each illustration, but remember that expense increases according to complexity, so the simplest level of presentation is best. Often, for the purpose of discussion, two simple figures with a few elements may be preferable to one figure with many elements.

Professional drafting services are usually used to produce a finished figure because most psychologists do not have the technical skill to produce a figure that meets printing requirements. However, any figure of professional *quality* is acceptable, whether drawn by a professional or by a person skilled in the use of press-on letters or other graphic aids. In any case, all figures must be in finished form ready for reproduction.

Computer-generated figures are acceptable. Submit them as glossy photographs, either in their original size or already reduced, as shown in Figure 1.

An author must obtain permission to reproduce a figure from a copyrighted source (see section 3.36).

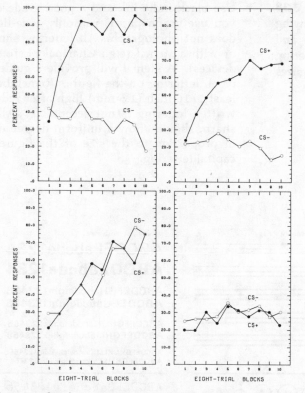

Figure 1. An example of a computer-generated figure. (Courtesy Michael J. Zajano and David A. Grant.)

**3.37
Size and
Proportion of
Figures**

Before drawing a figure, consider the complexity of the material, the page size, and the column width of the journal you are writing for. Figures should not be larger than 8½ × 11 inches (22 × 28 cm) or smaller than a single column width of the journal. Figures of equal importance should be of equal size. Ideally, figures should be drawn to journal page width or column width. If this is not possible, draw figures large, and the printer will photograph them in reduced proportions to fit the journal page.

As you construct a figure, consider what will happen to its various elements—the letters, numbers, lines, plot points, and spaces between and within curves—when reduced proportionally. These elements must be large enough in the original figure to be legible if reduced for printing. Figure 2 shows how reduction affects legibility of lettering and symbols frequently used in technical illustrations.

Figure 3 illustrates one method of estimating both dimensions of a figure after reduction. The outside rectangle represents the dimensions of the original illustration. A diagonal line forms the axis that a change in size will follow. The inside rectangle represents the figure reduced to three fourths of the original size. For estimating purposes, the diagonal line can be drawn on the back of the original illustration if the lines are penciled very lightly so no mark or impression shows through on the face of the copy. If it appears that the reduction would reduce legibility, the figure may have to be redrawn.

■ Use black india ink and a good grade of white drawing paper. If you use graph paper, use only blue-line grid paper because blue does not photograph. All lettering should be done professionally or with a stencil (e.g., Chartpak, Leroy, Wrico, or Ames lettering devices). A stencil will provide a guide to the size and proportion of all lettering on the figure. Remember that lettering must be at least 1/16 inch (1.5 mm) high after reduction. Freehand and type-written lettering is not acceptable. All lines should be clear and sharp, should show a uniform degree of blackness, and should be in proportion to the size of the figure. It is best not to use all capital lettering.

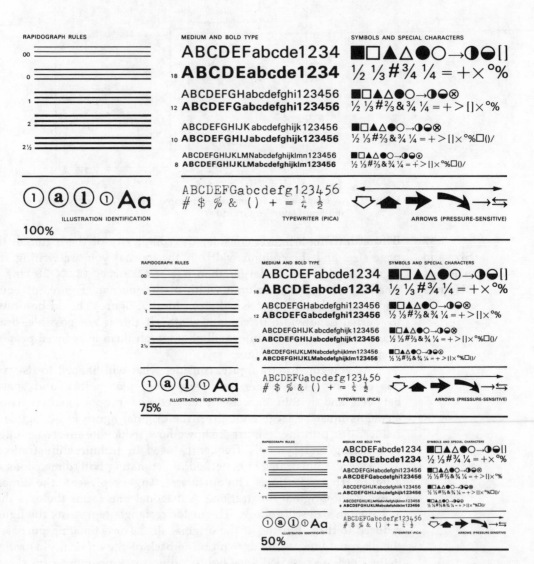

Figure 2. Letters and symbols frequently used in technical illustration. The top group shows actual copy size (100%), and the second and third groups show how 75% and 50% reductions affect legibility of original size.

52

- Use heavy lines for the vertical and horizontal axes. Usually, the independent variable is plotted on the horizontal axis and the dependent variable on the vertical axis.

- Clearly label the axis with both the quantity measured and the units in which it is measured.

- Place the legends parallel to the proper axes. The numbering and lettering of grid points should be horizontal for both axes.

- Use legibility as a guide in determining the number of curves to place on a figure. A good general rule is no more than four curves per figure. Allow adequate space between and within curves, particularly if the figure is to be reduced.

- Use distinct geometric forms, such as circles or squares, for plot points.

- In choosing a grid scale, consider the purpose of the figure, the range and scale separation to be used on both axes, and the overall dimensions of the figure, so that plotted curves span the entire illustration.

- Indicate scale values by grid marks placed on each axis at the appropriate intervals.

- Enclose figures with a box outline to set them off from the text.

- On the back of each figure, write *lightly* in pencil or felt-tip pen the article title and the figure number, and designate the top of the figure for spatial orientation. Also indicate which figures are comparable or of equal importance so that the printer may scale them appropriately.

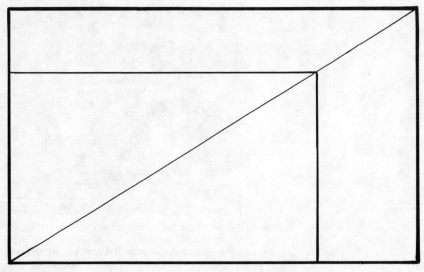

Figure 3. Use of the diagonal to estimate reduced dimensions of a figure. Proportions of an illustration do not change regardless of scale.

3.39
Reproducing
Photographs

Because reproduction tends to soften contrast and detail in photographs, it is important to start with rich contrast and sharp prints. All photographs should be professionally prepared with a background that produces the greatest amount of contrast. If it is necessary to retouch a photograph or apply arrows or letters, protect the retouched surface with a tissue overlay.

Do not use color slides for black-and-white reproduction. The transition from color to black and white is unpredictable and usually inaccurate in tone. If your only photograph is a color slide, have a 5 × 7 inch (12.7 × 17.8 cm) black-and-white print made to your satisfaction before submitting it for publication.

3.40
Photomicrographs

Photomicrographs are reproduced as halftones (see section 3.39 on reproducing photographs). Because they are illustrations that elaborate on the text rather than a presentation of new data, they should be cropped and arranged for the most economical use of space (see Figure 4). Location of electrode tips can often best be shown on a

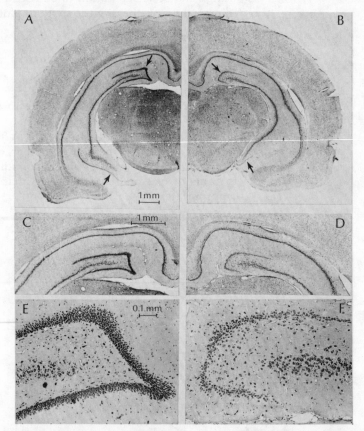

Figure 4. An example of a photomicrograph. (From "Effects of Hippocampal Granule-Cell Agenesis on Acquisition of Escape from Fear and One-Way Active-Avoidance Responses" by Steven J. Haggbloom, Robert L. Brunner, and Shirley A. Bayer, *Journal of Comparative and Physiological Psychology*, 1974, 83, 447–457. Copyright 1974 by the American Psychological Association. Reprinted by permission.)

schematic line drawing of a brain section with enough landmark structures shown and labeled to provide orientation for the reader. Also indicate the degree of magnification and the type of staining materials used.

3.41
Bar
Graphs

Bar graphs are visual representations of data that usually can be presented more economically in text or in a small table. When a bar graph is necessary, use the instructions for preparing figures.

3.42
Figure
Numbers

All graphs, charts, illustrations, and halftones are called figures when mentioned in text and captions. Number all figures consecutively with arabic numerals throughout an article (i.e., Figure 1, Figure 2). This number should be written lightly on the back of the figure, never on the face of the figure. In the text, refer to figures by their numbers:

`as shown in Figure 2, the relationships are`

`data are related (see Figure 2).`

Never say "the figure above/below" or "the figure on page 12" because the position and page number of a figure cannot be determined until the printer makes up the pages. However, indicate to the printer the approximate placement of each figure in text (see section 4.22 for instructions).

3.43
Figure
Captions

A good figure caption is concise but explanatory. It should describe the contents of the figure in a brief sentence or phrase:

Poor: `Responses.`   **Better:** `Mean percentage of reinforced`

`responses before and after`

`the experimental treatment.`

In parentheses after the figure caption, add any information needed to clarify the figure, such as an explanation of abbreviations or units of measurement. A reader should not have to refer to the text to decipher the figure.

Do not place the figure caption on the figure itself. Instead, list all figure captions, with their numbers, on a separate sheet (see section 4.21 for typing instructions).

3.44
Additional
Copies
of Figures

Submit the same number of copies of figures as the typewritten parts of the manuscript (see Table 15). The original figures must be prepared as outlined in this section; the duplicate figures may be photocopies. All figures should be submitted on 8½ × 11 inch (22 × 28 cm) paper to protect against loss; do not mount figures on cardboard.

Quotations

Like tables and figures, quotations support or elucidate text. Short quotations are incorporated in text and enclosed by double quotation marks. Longer quotations are set off from the text as a free-standing block with no quotation marks. Whether in text or block form, quotations may be shortened by the use of ellipses (see section 3.47) and paraphrase.

The following examples illustrate the application of APA style to quotations as described in this section (for detailed typing instructions, see section 4.12).

(3.45)   **(3.47)**

Quotation 1.   He stated, "The 'placebo effect' . . . disappeared when behaviors were studied in this manner" (Smith, 1964, p. 276), but he did not clarify which behaviors were studied.   **(3.46)**

Quotation 2.   Smith (1964) found that "the 'placebo effect,' which had been verified in previous studies, disappeared when [his own and others'] behaviors were studied in this manner" (p. 276).   **(3.48)** **(3.49)**

Quotation 3.   Smith (1964) found the following:

(3.46)

> The "placebo effect," which had been verified in previous studies, disappeared when behaviors were studied in this manner. Furthermore, the behaviors, both his own and others', were never exhibited again, even when real drugs were administered. (p. 276)

3.45 **Permissible** **Changes from** **Original** **Quotation**	The first letter of the first word in a quotation may be changed to a capital or small letter. The punctuation mark at the end of a sentence may be changed to fit the syntax. Any other changes (e.g., italicizing words for emphasis or omitting words) must be explicitly indicated by ellipses or bracketed explanations (see sections 3.47 and 3.48). Always check the typed copy with the original source to ensure that no other changes have been made. Interior punctuation, spelling, and wording must follow the original, even if it is incorrect.
3.46 **Double** **or Single** **Quotation** **Marks**	**In text.** Use *double* quotation marks for quotations in text. Use *single* quotation marks within double quotation marks to set off material that ordinarily uses double marks. **In block form.** Do not use *any* quotation marks to enclose block quotations. Use double quotation marks to enclose any quoted material within a block quotation.
3.47 **Omitted** **Material**	Three ellipsis points (. . .) are used to indicate omitted material within a sentence. Four points indicate any omission between two sentences within a quotation. Do not use ellipsis points at the beginning or end of a quotation.
3.48 **Inserted** **Material**	Brackets, not parentheses, are used to enclose material, including additions and explanations, inserted in a quotation by some person other than the original author.
3.49 **Citation** **of Source**	Always cite the source of a direct quotation. Include the author, year, and page number. Enclose the citation in parentheses. Depending on where the quotation falls, punctuation differs:

- If the quoted passage is in the middle of a sentence, end the passage with quotation marks, cite the source in parentheses immediately, and continue the sentence. Use no other punctuation unless the meaning of the sentence requires it. (See Quotation 1.)

- If the quoted passage falls at the end of a sentence, close the passage with quotation marks, cite the source in parentheses after the quotation marks, and end with the period or other punctuation outside the final parentheses. (See Quotation 2.)

- If the quoted passage is set off in a block (and therefore without quotation marks), cite the source in parentheses after the final period. (See Quotation 3.)

3.50 **Permission** **to Quote**	If you quote at length from a copyrighted work in material you intend to publish, you usually need written permission from the owner of the copyright. Permissible length of quoted material varies from one copyright owner to another. APA policy permits use of 500 words of text without explicit permission.

Reference Citations in Text

APA journals use the author–date method of citation; that is, the surname of the author and the year of publication are inserted in text at an appropriate point:

```
Smith (1970) compared reaction times
In a recent study of reaction times (Smith, 1970)
```

This method gives readers useful information in text and enables them to locate the citation easily in the alphabetical reference list.

As indicated in the first example, if the name of the author occurs in textual discussion, only the year of publication is cited in parentheses. Otherwise, both name and date appear in parentheses, separated by a comma (second example). In the rare case where both the year and author are given in text, no further reference is required:

```
In 1970, Smith compared
```

In continuous discussion on the same page, or even on the next pages, the name or study may be mentioned again without the parenthetical citation of the year if no ambiguity results.

**3.51
Two or
More
Authors**

If a work has two authors, always cite both names every time the reference occurs in text. If the work has more than two authors, cite all authors the first time the reference occurs; include only the surname of the first author followed by "et al." (not italicized) and the year in subsequent citations of the same reference:

```
Williams, Jones, and Smith (1963) found    (first occurrence)
Williams et al. (1963) found              (subsequent citations)
```

If, however, citation of two references in the same year shortens to the same form (e.g., Williams et al., 1963, for Williams, Jones, & Smith, 1963, and Williams, Smith, Jones, & Brown, 1963), always cite both in full to avoid confusion. (*Note:* All multiple-author citations in footnotes, tables, and figures should include surnames of all authors.)

If multiple-author citations occur in running text, the names are connected by "and." In parenthetical and tabular material, the names are joined by an ampersand (&):

```
as shown by Jones and Smith (1963).
as has been shown (Jones & Smith, 1963).
```

**3.52
No Author or
Corporate
Author**

If there is no author, in the text citation use the first two or three words of the entry in the reference list (usually the title):

```
with blind reviewing ("Eight APA Journals," 1972).
```

(See Example 6 in Appendix C for the reference list entry.)

If the author is a lengthy corporate name, the parenthetical text citation may be abbreviated unless the full name adds to the understanding of the text:

(NIMH, 1971)   (abbreviated in text)
National Institute of Mental Health
                              (corporate author in reference list)

As a general rule, give enough information in the text citation to locate the entry in the reference list without difficulty.

3.53
Authors with
Same Surname

If a reference list includes publications by two or more authors with the same surname, citations in text include their initials to avoid confusion, even if the year of publication differs.

3.54
Multiple
Citations

Multiple citations in parentheses at the same point in text follow the order of the reference list (see section 3.60). Therefore, multiple citations of the *same* author are arranged in *chronological* order, separated by commas, and the author's name is not repeated for each work. In citing more than one paper by the same author in one year, the suffixes a, b, c, etc., are added after the year, and the year is repeated. (These same suffixes are used in the reference list.) In-press citations come last.

Recent studies (Jones, 1956, 1958, 1966a, 1966b,
    in press-a, in press-b) have shown

If *different* authors are cited at the same point in text, the citations are arranged *alphabetically* by authors' surnames, separated by a semicolon, and enclosed in one pair of parentheses.

Recent studies (Brown & Smith, 1965; Smith, 1962,
    1964; Williams, 1971) have shown

3.55
Citation of a
Particular Part
of a Source

Citation of a particular page, chapter, figure, table, or equation should be made at the appropriate point in text rather than in the reference list. Because material within a book is often difficult to locate, authors should whenever possible give page numbers in books to assist readers. Page numbers are always given for quotations (see section 3.49). Note that *page* and *chapter* are abbreviated in such citations:

(Jones, 1958, pp. 10-19)
(Smith, 1960, chap. 3)

3.56
References in
Parenthetical
Material

When citations are within parenthetical material, use commas (not brackets) to set off the date:

(see Table 2 of Jones, 1973, for complete data)

Reference Lists

The reference list at the end of each journal article establishes the authority of the article by citing material publicly available. Authors should choose references judiciously and only include sources that readers may retrieve. Materials *not generally available* should be cited as reference *notes* (see sections 3.61 and 3.62).

3.57
Citation
in Text and
Reference List

A *reference list* cites works that specifically support a particular article. This is in contrast to a *bibliography*, which cites works for background or further reading. References cited in text must appear in the reference list, and conversely, each entry in the reference list must be cited in text. The author must make certain that references appear in both places and are in agreement. Failure to do so can result in expensive changes after a manuscript is set in type. The cost of these changes is borne by the author.

3.58
Accuracy
and
Completeness

Because one purpose of listing references is to enable readers to use them, reference data must be correct and complete. Each entry must contain all data necessary for identification and library search; therefore, the most important requirement in preparing a reference list is to check carefully against the original publication. Give special attention to spelling of proper names, spelling of words in foreign languages including accents or other special marks, and whether journal titles, years, volume numbers, and pages are complete. Authors are responsible for all information in a reference. Editors cannot complete an incomplete reference, and an inaccurate reference "will stand in print as an annoyance to future investigators and a monument to the writer's carelessness" (Bruner, 1942, p. 68).

3.59
APA Style

All references should be prepared in the style below. For examples of actual citations and further explanation, see Appendix C. Follow the style religiously; it is a good way to catch omissions and oversights. Because journal and copy editors cannot make major adjustments in format, they will return improperly prepared or incomplete references for repairs.

Sequence. Arrange the elements in a reference entry in the following order:

- Author: all authors of the work, with surnames and initials (not full name) in inverted order
- Title: article, chapter, or book
- Facts of publication:

    For journals—journal name in full, date of publication, volume number, inclusive pages

    For books—city of publication, publisher's name, publication date.

Punctuation. Use *periods* to separate the three major subdivisions of a reference citation: author, title, and publication data. Use *commas* within the subdivisions (e.g., between date and volume number in a journal entry). Use a *colon* between the place of publication and the book publisher. Use *parentheses* for extensions, qualifications, or interpretations of each subdivision or the entire entry. Punctuate accurately and uniformly, following the examples in Appendix C.

- Periods separate the subdivisions:

  ```
  Author, J. P. Title of the work. Publication data.
  ```

- Commas separate within subdivisions:

  Publication data for a journal

  ```
  American Psychologist, 1973, 28, 376-384.
  ```

  Publication data for a book

  ```
  Academic Press, 1972.
  ```

- A colon separates the place of publication and the publisher:

  ```
  New York: Academic Press, 1972.
  ```

- Parentheses extend, qualify, or interpret:

  Title entry

  ```
  Style manual (2nd ed.).
  ```

  Entire entry

  ```
  . . . 276-277. (Abstract)
  ```

Capitalization. Capitalize entries according to the following:

Journal titles: Capitalize the initial letter of all major words.

Article, chapter, or book titles: Capitalize the initial letter of the first word only. Make exceptions according to common usage, such as capital letters for proper names, German nouns, first word of a title within a title, and first word after a colon or dash.

Italics and quotes. Underline book and journal titles and journal volume numbers to indicate italics. Article and chapter titles are set in roman type without quotation marks.

Abbreviations. Titles of journals are not abbreviated; they are spelled out in full. Acceptable abbreviations in reference lists include:

chap.	chapter
ed.	edition
rev. ed.	revised edition
2nd ed.	second edition
Ed. (Eds.)	Editor(s)
p. (pp.)	page(s)
Vol.	Volume (as in Vol. 1)
vols.	volumes (as in 4 vols.)
No.	Number
Pt.	Part
Tech. Rep.	Technical Report
Suppl.	Supplement
trans.	translated by

Arabic numerals. Although some volume numbers of books and journals are given in roman numerals, APA journals use arabic numerals for all numbers in reference lists (e.g., Vol. 3, not Vol. III).

**3.60
Ordering
References
in the
Reference List**

Inverted order of names. List all names in inverted order, last name followed by the initial or initials (not full name). Each initial is followed by a period and a space:

Brown, J. R.

In the case of multiple authorship, use the inverted order for all names, separating each name from the preceding name with a comma. Use a comma and an ampersand (&) before the final name, even with two authors:

Brown, J. R., & Smith, D. F.

Brown, J. R., Smith, D. F., & Jones, K.

Alphabetizing names. Arrange entries in alphabetical order by the surname of the first author, using the following rules for special cases:

- Alphabetize letter by letter. However, remember that "nothing precedes something": Brown, J. R. precedes Browning, A. R., even though *i* precedes *j* in the alphabet.

- Alphabetize the prefixes M', Mc, and Mac literally, not as if they were spelled Mac: MacArthur precedes McAllister.

- Surnames that use articles and prepositions (de, la, du, von, etc.) are alphabetized according to different rules for different languages. If the prefix is commonly part of the surname (e.g., de Gaulle), alphabetize by prefix. If the prefix is not customarily used (e.g., Helmholtz, rather than von Helmholtz), disregard it in alphabetization. The biographical section of *Webster's New Collegiate Dictionary* is a helpful guide on foreign surnames.

Ordering several works by the same first author. When ordering several works by the same first author, repeat the author's name and use the following rules to arrange the entries:

- Single-author entries precede multiple-author entries beginning with the same name:

  Brown, J. R.

  Brown, J. R., & Smith, D. F.

- References with the same first author and different second or third authors are arranged alphabetically by the surname of the second author, etc.:

  Brown, J. R., Jones, K., & Smith, D. F.

  Brown, J. R., & Smith, D. F.

- Several references to the same author are arranged by year of publication, the earliest first:

  Brown, J. R. . . . 1967

  Brown, J. R. . . . 1970

- References to the same author published in the same year (or both in press) are arranged alphabetically by title (excluding *a* or *the*). Lowercase letters in parentheses—(a), (b), etc.—are placed after the final period of each entry:

  Brown, J. R. Control . . . 1970, <u>54</u>, 27–30. (a)

  Brown, J. R. Roles of . . . 1970, <u>96</u>, 45–78. (b)

Entries without personal author. Occasionally a work will have as its author an agency, association, or institution, or it will have no author at all.

- Alphabetize corporate authors, such as associations or government agencies, by the first significant word of the name. Full official names should be used (e.g., American Psychological Association, not APA). A parent body precedes a subdivision (e.g., University of Michigan, Department of Psychology).

- If, and only if, the work is signed "Anonymous," the entry begins with Anonymous spelled out and is alphabetized as if Anonymous were a true name.

- If there is no author, the title moves to the author position, and the entry is alphabetized by the first significant word of the title.

Entries not numbered. In APA style, entries are *not* numbered. However, some non-APA journals number entries and cite the numbers as references in text.

Reference Notes

It is sometimes necessary to cite material that is not widely and easily available, for example, reports of limited circulation, unpublished works, personal communications, papers presented at meetings, symposia, some technical reports, and works in progress. Restrict the use of such material to the works that are absolutely essential to the article, and list each work in a section of reference notes, not as footnotes or in the reference list. Cite all notes in text (see section 3.62).

3.61 Style

Because material in the notes varies, it is impossible to state precise style rules. In general, give as much information about a study as possible: author, title, and date (always give the year, the month if known), the address from which the material may be obtained, and any official number. Include any additional information necessary to explain the source.

Follow basic rules for APA references in formulating notes (see section 3.59). Number and list notes in the order in which they are cited in text. Follow the examples in Table 10 for the more common types.

3.62 Citation in Text

Notes should be cited in text in the same way as references, with one minor variation; the word Note and the number replace the date:

Jones (Note 1)

(Jones, Note 1)

When notes and references appear together, list references first in alphabetical order; place notes after the references in numerical order. Separate the notes from the references by a semicolon.

(Jones, 1958; Miller, 1949; Smith, Note 2; Brown, Note 4)

Table 10: Examples of Reference Notes

Kind of note	Typewritten example	Comment
Unpublished manuscript not submitted for publication	1. Hollingshead, A. B. Two-factor index of social position. Unpublished manuscript, 1957. (Available from [author's address]).	
Unpublished manuscript submitted for publication but not yet accepted	2. Jones, J. S., & Smith, F. D. Psychological advantages of the four-day workweek. Manuscript submitted for publication, 1974.	Do not give name of journal to which article has been submitted.
Unpublished manuscript with a university cited	3. Walker, K. E., & Woods, M. E. Time use for care of family members (Use-of-Time Research Project, Working Paper 1). Unpublished manuscript, Cornell University, 1972.	These may or may not be available from a university and are considered limited-circulation works.
Book in preparation but not yet accepted by a publisher	4. Brown, S. Cognitive development and learning. Book in preparation, 1974.	(Continued)

Table 10—Continued

Kind of note	Typewritten example	Comment
Government report with no National Technical Information Service (NTIS) number and unavailable from the Government Printing Office (GPO)	5. Play, J. A., & Hardacre, L. W. <u>Age, years of schooling, and intelligence as predictors of military effectiveness for Naval enlistees</u> (Report No. 65-19). San Diego, Calif.: U.S. Navy Medical Neuropsychiatry Research Unit, July 1965.	If a government report is available from NTIS or from GPO, give the appropriate information and cite in the reference list (see Examples 28 and 29, Appendix C).
Technical report from a university (usually under government contract) with no NTIS number	6. Galanter, E., & Jacobs, D. E. <u>A comparison of category scaling methods</u> (Tech. Rep. PLR-28). New York: Columbia University, Psychophysics Laboratory, February 1973.	
Research report available on a limited basis only from its source	7. Stewart, N. <u>Creativity: A literature survey</u> (ETS RM 53-08). Princeton, N.J.: Educational Testing Service, 1953.	Unpublished reports unavailable on a continuing basis from an organization or agency cannot be included in the reference list.

Table 10—Continued

Kind of note	Typewritten example	Comment
Paper presented at a meeting	8. Zedeck, S., & Baker, H. T. <u>Evaluation of behavioral expectation scales</u>. Paper presented at the meeting of the Midwestern Psychological Association, Detroit, May 1971.	Give state name if the city is not well known.
Contribution to a symposium	9. Bugental, D. E. Inconsistency between verbal and nonverbal components in parental communication patterns: Its interpretation and effects. In P. Zimbardo (Chair), <u>Consistency as a process and a problem in psychology.</u> Symposium presented at the meeting of the International Congress of Psychology, Tokyo, 1972.	
Personal communication	10. Barnes, J. Personal communication, July 18, 1970.	Give as exact a date as possible.

Footnotes

3.63
Kinds of
Footnotes

APA journals use four kinds of footnotes, each serving a different purpose:

Acknowledgment and author identification. Standard footnotes of acknowledgment and author identification appear on the first page of an article. These notes should:

- acknowledge the basis of a study (e.g., doctoral dissertation or paper presented at a meeting)
- acknowledge a grant or other financial support
- acknowledge scholarly review or assistance in conducting the study or preparing the manuscript
- elaborate on the author's affiliation or note a change in affiliation
- designate the address of the author to whom requests for reprints or inquiries should be sent.

Content footnotes. Content footnotes are explanations or amplifications of the text. Because they are distracting to readers and expensive to include in printed material, an author should consider whether such footnotes strengthen the discussion. In most cases, an article is best integrated by including important information in the text and omitting irrelevant information.

Rather than footnoting long or complicated material, such as proofs or derivations unnecessary to the text, consider (a) indicating in a short footnote that the material is available from the author, (b) depositing the material in a national retrieval center and including an appropriate footnote (see Appendix A, NAPS), or (c) adding an appendix (see section 1.10). If an appendix is used, the reference in text should read:

`(see Appendix A for complete derivation).`

Reference footnotes. Footnotes are rarely used in APA articles for reference purposes. Citations for material of limited availability should appear in the Reference Notes section (see sections 3.61 and 3.62). Acceptable reference footnotes include:

- legal citations, which should follow the footnote style of *A Uniform System of Citation* (1967) published by the Harvard Law Review Association
- copyright permission footnotes (see section 3.36 for the form for citing reprinted material—text, tables, or figures).

Table footnotes. Table footnotes are appended only to a specific table (see section 3.33).

3.64
Numbering
of Footnotes

Footnotes of acknowledgment and author identification *are not numbered*. In the past, these footnotes were attached by superscript numbers to the title and author's name, but because they are a standard part of every article, both in nature and position, they are no longer numbered.

Text footnotes should be numbered consecutively throughout the article with superscript arabic numerals. If, after a footnote occurs it is later mentioned, use a parenthetical note "(see Footnote 3)," rather than the superscript number. (See section 4.19 for detailed typing instructions on footnotes.)

Footnotes to a table should be *lettered* consecutively *within* each table with superscript lowercase letters (see section 3.33).

Punctuation

3.65
Period

See the following sections for discussion of periods used as other than terminal punctuation: abbreviations (3.5), quotations (3.47), and references (3.59).

3.66
Comma

Use a comma:

- before *and* and *or* in a series of three or more

  the height, width, or depth

  in a study by Thomas, Beck, and Gilbert (1964)

- to set off a nonessential or nonrestrictive clause, that is, a clause that the sentence can do without

  the switch, which was on a panel, controlled

- to separate two independent clauses joined by a conjunction, especially if the clauses are lengthy

  The floor was covered with cedar shavings, and paper was available for shredding and nest building.

Do not use a comma:

- before an essential or restrictive clause, that is, a clause that identifies, limits, or defines the word it modifies

  the switch that stops the recording device also controlled

- between the two parts of a compound predicate

  The results were not in agreement with Smith's hypothesis and indicated that the effect of intervening problems was nonsignificant.

3.67
Semicolon

Use a semicolon:

- to separate two independent clauses that are not joined by a conjunction

  The subjects in the first study were unpaid
      volunteers; those in the second study were paid
      for their participation.

- to separate items that already contain commas

  The color order was red, white, blue; blue,
      white, red; or white, red, blue.

  (Adams & Baker, 1964; Jones, 1963)

  F (1, 188) = 9.76, p < .01; F (16, 188) = 1.68,
      p > .05

3.68
Colon

Use a colon:

- before a final phrase or clause that illustrates, extends, or amplifies preceding material (if the final clause is a complete sentence, it begins with a capital letter)

  They have agreed on the outcome: Informed subjects
      perform better than do uninformed subjects.

  The digits were shown in the following order:
      3, 2, 4, 1.

- in ratios and proportions

  The proportions (salt:water) were 1:8, 1:4,
      and 1:2.

- in references between place of publication and publisher

  New York: Wiley, 1958.

3.69
Hyphen

See section 3.75 on hyphenation.

3.70
Dash

Use the dash only to indicate a sudden interruption in the continuity of a sentence. Overuse weakens flow of material.

When there are two psychologists of the same name--
    one male, one female--and research is cited by
    use of the last name only,

3.71
Quotation
Marks

See section 3.46 for discussion of double and single quotation marks with material quoted directly from a source. Observe the following guidelines for other uses of double quotation marks:

70

Use double quotation marks:

- to introduce a word or phrase used in a special way, that is, ironic usage, slang, or an invented or coined phrase. Use quotation marks the first time the word or phrase is used; they are not necessary thereafter.

  ```
  for the four "less than" comparative items
  the "bad guy" variable
  ```

  Do not misuse quotation marks to hedge or to apologize for using a given expression.

- to reproduce material from a test item or verbatim instructions to subjects

  ```
  The first fill-in item was "could be expected
      to _____."
  ```

  If instructions are long, set them off from text in a block format without quotation marks.

  ```
  In the negative condition, the question read,
      It is necessary for us to know whether
      the people who participate in this
      experiment had any information about
      its nature beforehand.  Of course we
      hope that you did not know anything
      about it.  Had you heard anything
      about this experiment before you
      participated in it?
  ```

  (*Note:* This block quotation would be typed double-spaced in a manuscript; see section 4.12 for typing instructions.)

**3.72
Parentheses**

Use parentheses:

- to set off structurally independent elements

  ```
  were significant (see Figure 5).
  ```

- to set off references within text

  ```
  Smith and Jones (1970) have reported
  is fully described elsewhere (James &
      Nelson, 1965)
  ```

- to explain an abbreviation

  ```
  effect on the galvanic skin response (GSR)
  ```

- to set off letters in a series

  ```
  The three measures were (a). . ., (b). . .,
      and (c). . . .
  ```

- to group mathematical expressions

$$(\underline{k} - 1)/(\underline{q} - 2)$$

- to enclose the citation of a direct quotation

"when behaviors were studied" (p. 276).

- to enclose enumeration of displayed formulas and equations

$$\underline{n} = \underline{c} + \underline{i} \qquad\qquad (1)$$

**3.73
Brackets**

Use brackets:

- to enclose parenthetical material within parentheses

(The results for the control group [$\underline{n}$ = 8] are also given in Figure 2.)

Exception 1: Do not use brackets if the material can be set off easily with commas: (as Smith, 1970, later concluded).

Exception 2: The order of brackets within parentheses is not applicable to mathematical material (see section 3.16).

- to enclose material inserted in a quotation by some person other than the original writer

"when [his own and others'] behaviors were studied" (p. 276).

Spelling

**3.74
Preferred
Spelling**

Webster's New Collegiate Dictionary (1973) is used by the APA journals as the standard spelling reference. If a word is not in the *Collegiate*, consult the more comprehensive *Webster's Third New International Dictionary* (1971). If the dictionary gives a choice, use the first spelling listed, for example, *aging* and *canceled* rather than *ageing* and *cancelled*.

**3.75
Hyphenation**

Most other spelling questions are concerned with compound words, that is, two words that may be written as (a) one unbroken word, (b) a hyphenated word, or (c) two separate words. Should it be *agemate, age-mate,* or *age mate*? The dictionary answers many such questions (it is *age-mate* in this case), especially for nonscientific words. But, because the language is constantly expanding, especially in science, dictionaries may not include an authoritative spelling for the new compounds common to science. If a compound is *not* in the dictionary, the APA journals follow the general principles of hyphenation given here and in Table 13.

General principle 1. Do not use a hyphen unless it serves a purpose. That is, if the meaning of a compound adjective is clear, a hyphen is not necessary. This is especially true of words used frequently in psychology.

```
least squares solution
semantic differential technique
```

General principle 2. When an invented or temporary compound is used as an adjective before a noun, it is sometimes hyphenated to avoid ambiguity. For example, are *different word lists* (a) lists composed of different words or (b) word lists that are different from other word lists? A properly placed hyphen helps the reader understand the intended meaning.

General principle 3. Most adjective rules are appropriate only when the compound adjective *precedes* the noun. If a compound adjective *follows* the noun, relationships are sufficiently clear without the hyphen.

```
client-centered counseling, but the counseling
  was client centered
t-test results, but results from t tests
```

General principle 4. Words formed with prefixes are usually written as one word, as in Table 11. Some exceptions, in Table 12, require hyphens.

General principle 5. When two or more modifiers have a common base, this base is sometimes omitted in all except the last modifier, but the hyphens are retained.

```
long- and short-term memory
2-, 3-, and 10-minute trials
```

Table 11: Words With Prefixes Written Without Hyphens

Prefix	Example	Prefix	Example
after	aftereffect	post	posttest
anti	antisocial	pre	preexperimental
bi	bilingual	pro	prowar
co	coeducation	pseudo	pseudoscience
counter	counterbalance	re	resensitize
extra	extracurricular	semi	semidarkness
infra	infrared	sub	subtest
inter	interstimulus	super	superordinate
intra	intraspecific	supra	supraliminal
multi	multiphase	ultra	ultrahigh
non	nonsignificant	un	unbiased
over	overaggressive	under	underdeveloped

Table 12: Words with Prefixes Written with Hyphens

Occurrence	Example
When the base word is	
capitalized	`pro-Freudian`
a number	`post-1960`
an abbreviation	`pre-UCS trial`
more than one word	`non-achievement-oriented` `students`

To clarify spelling and meaning	`re-pair (pair again)`
	`re-form (form again)`
	`un-ionized`

To avoid awkward double vowels	`anti-intellectual` `co-occur`
To avoid possible misreading	`co-worker`

Table 13: Guide to Hyphenating Psychological Terms

Rule	Example
Hyphenate:	

1. A compound with a participle when it precedes the noun it modifies	`role-playing technique`
	`anxiety-arousing condition`
	`water-deprived animals`

2. A phrase used as an adjective when it precedes the noun it modifies	`trial-by-trial analysis`
	`to-be-recalled items`
	`all-or-none questionnaire`

3. An adjective and noun compound when it precedes and modifies another noun	`high-anxiety group`
	`middle-class families`
	`low-frequency words`

4. All *self-* compounds whether they are adjectives or nouns	`self-report technique`
	`the test was self-paced`
	`self-esteem`

5. A compound with a number as the first element when the compound precedes a noun	`two-way analysis of variance`
	`six-trial problem`
	`12th-grade students`

(Continued)

Table 13—Continued

Rule	Example
Do not hyphenate:	
6. A compound using an adverb ending in *-ly*	widely used test relatively homogeneous sample randomly assigned subjects
7. A compound using a comparative or superlative adjective	better written paper less informed interviewers higher scoring students
8. Chemical terms	sodium chloride solution amino acid compound
9. Foreign phrases used as adjectives	a posteriori test laissez faire policy *but:* ad-lib feeding (see *Webster's*)
10. A modifier using a letter or numeral as the second element	Group B subjects Type II error Trial 1 performance

Capitalization

Do capitalize:

- nouns followed by numerals or letters that denote a specific place in a numbered series

  on Day 2 of Experiment 4
  during Trial 5, Group B performed
  as seen in Table 2 and Figure 6

  Exceptions: page 1   row 3
                chapter 4   column 5

- trade and brand names of drugs, equipment, and food

  Hunter Klockounter
  Plexiglas
  Purina Lab Chow

- factors within a factor analysis

  the Activity factor

- exact, complete test titles as published

  the Advanced Vocabulary Test

  Minnesota Multiphasic Personality Inventory

  Stroop Color-Word Interference Test

- names of university departments only if they refer to a specific department within a specific university

  Department of Sociology, University of Washington

- major words in titles of books and journal articles in text but not in reference lists. Conjunctions, articles, and short prepositions are not considered major words.

  In his book, <u>History of Psychology</u>

  The criticism of the article "Attitudes Toward
      Mental Health Workers"

- first word after a colon or dash when the word begins a subtitle or a complete sentence (see section 3.68 for an example)

- major words in article headings (see section 4.16 for examples)

- first word in table heads and major words in table titles (see Tables 8 and 9 for examples).

Do not capitalize:

- names of effects in an analysis of variance

  a significant age effect
  main effect of serial position

- names of conditions or groups in an experiment

  experimental and control groups
  subjects were divided into information and
      no-information conditions

- nouns that precede a variable

  trial <u>n</u>   item <u>x</u>

- laws, theories, and hypotheses

  Gregory's theory of illusions
  the empirical law of effect

- shortened or inexact titles of tests or titles of unpublished tests

  a vocabulary test
  Stroop color test

Italics

3.77
Italics
Words underlined in a manuscript appear in italics in print. In general, italics are used infrequently. For specific use in APA journals, see Table 14. When in doubt, do not underline, because it is easier to add than to delete underlines at the copy-editing stage.

Table 14: Use of Italics

Rule	Typewritten example	Printed example
Use italics for:		
1. Titles of books, periodicals, and microfilm publications	<u>Words into Type</u> <u>American Psychologist</u>	*Words into Type* *American Psychologist*
2. Genera, species, and varieties	<u>Macaca mulatta</u>	*Macaca mulatta*
3. Introduction of new, technical, or key term	The term <u>backward masking</u>	The term *backward masking*
4. Letter, word, phrase, or sentence cited as a linguistic example	words such as <u>big</u> and <u>little</u> the letter <u>a</u>	words such as *big* and *little* the letter *a*
5. Letters used as statistical symbols or algebraic variables	$\underline{F}$ (1, 53) = 10.03 $\underline{t}$ test trial $\underline{n}$ $\underline{a}/\underline{b} = \underline{c}/\underline{d}$	F (1, 53) = 10.03 t test trial n $a/b = c/d$
6. Some test scores and scales	Rorschach scores: <u>F%</u>, <u>Z</u> MMPI scales: <u>Hs</u>, <u>Pd</u>	Rorschach scores: *F%*, *Z* MMPI scales: *Hs*, *Pd*
7. Hullian symbols	$\underline{r}_G$; $\underline{r}_F$	r_G; r_F
8. Volume number in reference list	1973, <u>26</u>, 46–67.	1973, *26*, 46–67.
Do not use italics for:		
9. Foreign words and abbreviations common in English	a posteriori a priori ad lib et al. per se vis-à-vis	a posteriori a priori ad lib et al. per se vis-à-vis

(Continued)

Table 14—Continued

Rule	Typewritten example	Printed example
10. Chemical terms	NaCl, LSD	NaCl, LSD
11. Trigonometric terms	sin, tan, log	sin, tan, log
12. Greek letters	χ (chi)	χ (chi)
13. Mere emphasis (permissible if emphasis might otherwise be lost; syntax and diction should provide emphasis)	It is <u>important</u> to bear in mind that <u>this</u> process is <u>not</u> proposed as a <u>stage</u> theory of development. [not acceptable]	It is *important* to bear in mind that *this* process is *not* proposed as a *stage* theory of development. [not acceptable]
14. Letters used as abbreviations	intertrial interval (ITI)	intertrial interval (ITI)

4 Typing, Mailing, and Proofreading

GENERAL TYPING INSTRUCTIONS

TYPING THE PARTS OF A MANUSCRIPT

SUBMITTING THE MANUSCRIPT

PROOFREADING

SAMPLE PAPER

4 Typing, Mailing, and Proofreading

The physical appearance of a manuscript is important. To editors and reviewers, a well-prepared manuscript looks professional. Careful preparation can prevent misinterpretation of content because of mechanical shortcomings and may influence a reviewer's decision positively. Once accepted for publication, a properly prepared manuscript facilitates the work of the copy editor and the printer and, thus, makes the manuscript more economical to publish. Poorly prepared copy may lead, at worst, to rejection of the manuscript and, at best, to delays, errors, additional cost, and aggravation.

Because the author is responsible for the correct presentation of his paper, he should prepare the material for the typist exactly as it is to be typed. The typist is responsible only for accurate transcription and mechanical details, such as spacing and general appearance. This chapter is designed to help the typist with these details. Because in some cases the typist may need additional information, the material here is cross-referenced with other parts of the Manual, primarily the sections on APA style. The sample paper at the end of this chapter shows how a properly typed manuscript should look.

After the manuscript is typed, the author should proofread it carefully, making all corrections and changes before submitting it for publication. Finally, the author should review the checklist on the inside back cover of this Manual. The completed manuscript should "attest not only to the typist's skill but to the author's concern about the accuracy and grace of his finished work as well as his awareness of the requirements of the publishing process" (University of Chicago Press *Manual of Style*, 1969, p. 34).

General Typing Instructions

**4.1
Paper**
Type the manuscript on one side of heavy, white bond paper. Do not use onionskin or erasable paper because these papers do not withstand handling, and the type blurs and becomes impossible to read.

Use standard-size paper ($8\frac{1}{2} \times 11$ inches [22×28 cm]). All pages of one manuscript must be the same size. Do not use half sheets or strips of paper glued, taped, or stapled to the pages; these are often torn off or lost in shipment and handling.

4.2 **Double-Spacing**	Double-space between *all* lines of the manuscript without exception. Double-spacing is essential for maximum legibility and for editorial marking and corrections. Double-spacing means leaving a double space after every line in the title, headings, footnotes, quotations, references, figure captions, and all parts of tables. **Set the typewriter for double-spacing and keep it there!**
4.3 **Margins**	Leave margins of 1–1½ inches (2½–4 cm) at the top, bottom, right, and left of every page to allow for editorial instructions and queries. Six inches (15 cm) is the best length for each typed line. Set a pica typewriter for a 60-character line and an elite machine for 72 characters. (Elite is the smaller of the two most common typefaces and is more widely used than pica type.) Uniform margins help the copy editor to estimate the length of an article.
4.4 **Paragraphs**	Indent five spaces for the first line of every paragraph, including each footnote, figure caption, and table footnote. Type the remaining lines of the manuscript to a uniform left-hand margin. The only exceptions to this rule are (a) the abstract, typed without paragraph indentation; (b) block quotations (see section 4.12); (c) headings (see section 4.16); and (d) entries in the reference list (see section 4.18).
4.5 **Pages**	**Separate pages.** Begin each of the following parts of the manuscript on a new page and arrange the pages as follows:

Cover page with title and author's name and affiliation (separate page)

Abstract (separate page)

Pages of text

Reference notes (start on a new page)

References (start on a new page)

Footnotes (start on a new page)

Tables (each on a separate page)

Figure captions (start on a new page)

Figures (each on a separate page)

This arrangement is not the way the printed article will appear; it is necessary for handling by the copy editor and the printer.

Numbering and identifying pages. After the pages are arranged in the above order, number them consecutively, beginning with the abstract page. Place the numbers in the upper right-hand corner using arabic numerals. Note that in addition to text pages, the abstract, reference, footnote, table, and figure caption pages are numbered. Only the cover sheet and figures are not numbered. If a page must be inserted or removed after numbering is completed, renumber the pages; do not number inserted pages with "6a" or make other repairs.

Occasionally pages are separated during the editorial process, so identify each manuscript page (except the cover page) by typing the first two or three words from the title in the upper right-hand corner above the page number. (Do *not* use the author's name to identify each page; it must be removed if the manuscript is blind reviewed.)

4.6
Corrections

Keep corrections to a minimum. Correct neatly. Acceptable methods of correction include:

- using correction paper, fluid, or tape to type over the error
- inserting a correction, either typed or printed in pencil, directly above the word or line to be corrected (not in the margin).

Unacceptable methods of correction include:

- writing vertically in the margin
- striking over a letter
- typing inserts on slips attached to pages
- writing illegibly or with a pen
- writing on the back of pages.

If many corrections occur on a page, retype the page.

4.7
Number of Copies

Prepare manuscripts in duplicate or triplicate (see Table 15 for individual journal requirements). One copy must be an *original* typewritten copy. This copy is marked by the copy editor and used by the printer; it must withstand repeated handling. The other copy or copies are used for editorial review; these may be machine copies (such as Xerox) if the image is clear and the paper is of good quality. In general, good machine copies are preferable to carbon copies. Each copy of the manuscript must be complete with figures and tables, although duplicate figures need not be glossy photographs. Retain one copy of the complete manuscript for reference and to guard against loss in the mail.

4.8
Typing Capitals

When the instructions state, "Type in capital and lowercase letters," they mean capitalize *only* initial letters of important words.

4.9
Spacing with Punctuation

Space after punctuation as follows:
- one space after commas and semicolons
- two spaces after colons, except in ratios (6:1)
- two spaces after periods ending sentences or parts of a reference citation
- one space after the periods of the initials in personal names (J. R. Jones)
- no space after internal periods in abbreviations (i.e., a.m., U.S.).

Quotation marks. When a period or comma occurs with a closing quotation mark, place the period or comma before, rather than after, the quotation mark. Put other punctuation inside quotation marks only when it is part of the quoted material.

```
At the beginning of each trial, the experimenter
   said, "This is a new trial."
```

```
Did the experimenter forget to say, "This is a
   new trial"?
```

Parentheses. If the context requires a comma (such as this), the comma follows a parenthesis. (If a complete sentence, like this one, is enclosed in parentheses, the period is placed inside the final parenthesis.) The period follows a parenthesis that falls at the end of a sentence (like this).

See sections 3.65–3.73 for additional instructions on punctuation.

Hyphens, dashes, and minus signs are each typed differently. Use no space before or after a hyphen. Type a dash as two hyphens with no space before or after. A minus sign is a hyphen with space on both sides.

```
hyphen:  trial-by-trial analysis
dash:    Studies--published and unpublished--are
minus:   (a - b)/c
```

Incorporate short quotations of fewer than four typewritten lines in the running text and enclose with double quotation marks (''). Set off longer quotations in a block with no quotation marks. In print, block quotations appear in reduced type, but when typing a long quotation, do not single-space to signify reduced type; rather, space for a new paragraph, indent, and type the entire quotation on the indented margin without the usual opening paragraph indentation. If the quotation is more than one paragraph, indent from the new margin. (See page 56 for typed examples of quotations in text and block quotations.)

Within a block quotation, use double quotation marks to enclose quoted material. In a quotation in running text that is already enclosed in double quotation marks, use single quotation marks to enclose quoted material.

Ellipsis points, used to indicate omitted material, are typed as three periods . . . separated from each other and the preceding and following text by spaces. Any omission between two sentences within a quotation is indicated by four dots (literally a period followed by three spaced dots. . . .).

Use brackets (hand-drawn brackets are acceptable), not parentheses, to enclose material inserted in a quotation by some person other than the original writer.

Typing the Parts of a Manuscript

4.13 Cover Sheet

The cover sheet includes three elements: the title, author and affiliation, and running head. (If the paper is to be blind reviewed, place footnotes that identify the author on the cover sheet. The cover sheet is removed by the editor prior to review.)

Title. Type the title in capital and lowercase letters, centered on the page. If the title is more than one line, double-space between the lines.

Author and affiliation. Type the name of the author in capital and lowercase letters, centered, one double-spaced line below the title. Type the institutional affiliation on the next double-spaced line. If the author's department is not a department of psychology, include the name of the department. If the affiliation is not a college or university, include the city and state:

John C. Jones

American Institutes for Research, Washington, D.C.

If two or more authors are at the same institution, type their names on one line if space permits. Commas separate the names of three or more authors. Their institutional affiliation appears on the next double-spaced line, just as it would for one author:

Nancy Smith, John Jones, and William Brown

University of Colorado

For multiple authors from different institutions, type the names on separate lines. Double-space between all lines. Examples of such settings follow:

Two authors, two affiliations:	*Three authors, two affiliations:*
John Jones	Roger Jones and John Smith
University of Maryland	University of Colorado
William Brown	Nancy Smith
American University	Stanford University

Running head. The author should supply a shortened title (maximum of 60 spaces including punctuation and space between words) to be used as a running head for the printed article. Type the running head at the bottom of the cover sheet in capital and lowercase letters.

4.14 Abstract

Begin the abstract on a new page. Type the word "Abstract" in capital and lowercase letters, centered, at the top of the page. The abstract is typed as a single paragraph in block format (i.e., without paragraph indentation).

4.15 Text Pages

Begin the text on a new page. Type the title of the paper at the top of the page and continue with the text. Do not start a new page when a heading occurs; the sections of the text follow each other without a break. For example, do not begin the method section on a new page.

4.16 Headings and Seriation

Headings. Headings are typed in the following manner:

<u>An Example of a Main Heading</u>

Main headings are centered, and the initial letters of main words are capitalized. The heading is underlined, and no period is used at the end.

<u>An Example of a Side Heading</u>

Side headings are typed flush to the left margin with the initial letters of main words capitalized. These headings are also underlined. Text follows on the next double-spaced line starting with a paragraph indentation.

<u>An example of a paragraph heading.</u> Paragraph headings, also known as "run-in sideheads," are typed with paragraph indentation. Capitalize only the initial letter of the first word, and underline the entire heading. End the heading with a period and two spaces, and start the text on the same line.

If a fourth level of heading is necessary start with a centered heading typed in all capital letters and follow with the three levels of headings shown above (see example in section 3.2).

Seriation. Seriation *within* a paragraph or sentence is shown by lowercase letters (not underlined) in parentheses:

(a) . . . , (b) . . . , and (c) . . . .

To indicate seriation *of* paragraphs (e.g., itemized conclusions or successive steps in a procedure), number each paragraph with an arabic numeral, followed by a period but not enclosed in or followed by parentheses:

1. Begin with paragraph indentation. Type

second and succeeding lines flush left.

2. The second item begins a new paragraph . . . .

4.17 Reference Notes

Start the notes on a separate sheet of paper. Type "Reference Notes" ("Reference Note," in the case of only one) in capital and lowercase letters, centered, at the top of the page.

Double-space all notes and type them in the order of their appearance in text. Type an arabic numeral followed by a period and two spaces before each entry. Align the second and succeeding lines with the first letter of the first line. (See section 3.61 for more detailed information and Table 10 for examples of reference notes.)

4.18
References

Start the reference list on a separate sheet of paper. Type the word "References" ("Reference," in the case of only one) in capital and lowercase letters, centered, at the top of the page.

Double-space all reference entries. (Although some theses and dissertations use single-spaced reference lists, single-spacing is *not* acceptable for manuscripts submitted to journals because it does not allow space for copy editing and printer's marks.) Type the first line of each entry flush left; indent second and succeeding lines three spaces. (See section 3.59 for more detailed information and Appendix C for examples of reference citations.)

4.19
Footnotes

In text, footnotes are numbered consecutively throughout the article with superscript arabic numerals. Type footnote numbers slightly above the line, like this,[1] *following* any punctuation mark except a dash. (*Note:* The superscript number falls inside a closing parenthesis if it applies only to matter within the parentheses.)

Type all text footnotes double-spaced on a separate sheet. Type the word "Footnotes" in capital and lowercase letters, centered, at the top of the page. Indent each footnote like a paragraph and type in the order of appearance in the text. See that all footnotes (*except* acknowledgment and identification notes) have a superscript number corresponding to a superscript number in the text. These numbers show the printer where to place the footnotes when he makes up pages.

If the paper is to be blind reviewed, type the author identification footnotes on the cover sheet (see section 4.13).

4.20
Tables

In text, indicate the position of each table by a clear break in the text, with instructions set off by lines above and below:

Insert Table 1 about here

Type each table double-spaced on a separate page. Center the word "Table" and its arabic numeral at the top of the page. On the next double-spaced line, center the table title, capitalizing the initial letters of the principal words. If the title contains more than one line or if there is a subtitle, double-space between lines and center each line. Center column headings and stubheadings within the table, capitalizing only the initial letter of the first words. Allow generous spacing between columns, and align material in each column (e.g., align decimal points). Type all footnotes with paragraph indentation, double-spaced, at the foot of the table. (For more detailed information on table footnotes, see section 3.33.) Rule each table in light pencil only if necessary to clarify divisions. Make *no* heavy or type-written rules, and do not use any rules for short and simple tables. (See Table 9 for an example of a well-typed table.)

4.21
Figure
Captions

The numbers and captions for figures are never lettered on the figure itself. Type the numbers and captions of all figures together on a separate sheet; this page is labeled "Figure Captions," typed in capital and lowercase letters, centered, at the top of the page. Begin each caption with paragraph indentation, and type the word "Figure," followed by the appropriate number, a period, and the caption. Capitalize only the first letter of the first word of a caption. If more than one line is required, double-space between lines.

4.22
Figures

In the text, show the location of each figure in the following way:

Insert Figure 1 about here

On the back of every figure, write *lightly* in pencil or felt-tip pen the article title (not the author's name) and the figure number, and indicate the top of the figure. These entries identify the figure for the printer. Be careful that the writing does not affect the front of the figure. All figures should be submitted on 8½ × 11 inch (22 × 28 cm) paper; do not mount figures on cardboard.

Submitting the Manuscript

4.23
Cover
Letter

Enclose a short cover letter when submitting a manuscript. Give the editor general information about the manuscript (e.g., whether it has been presented at a scientific meeting) as well as specific details, such as the number of tables and figures. Enclose a copy of the permission letter for any copyrighted material that you are reproducing. Include a telephone number and address for future correspondence.

4.24
Wrapping
and
Shipping

Do not bind or staple the pages together. Editors and printers prefer to work with loose sheets held together by a paper clip.

To protect the manuscript from rough handling in the mail, use a strong envelope stiffened with cardboard or corrugated filler if drawings or photographs are enclosed. If the manuscript is heavy, protect it further with a string tied securely around the envelope.

Submit the manuscript in triplicate (duplicate for some journals; see Table 15). Keep one copy of the complete manuscript for reference and to guard against loss in the mail.

Mail the manuscript first-class to the editor, not to the APA journal office. Because editors and their addresses change, always check the most recent issue of a journal to ascertain the current editor's name and address.

4.25
Future
Correspondence

After a paper has been accepted and scheduled for publication, send correspondence about proofs and other production matters to the Executive Editor, Journal Office, APA, 1200 17th Street, N.W., Washington, D.C. 20036. Send correspondence concerning any necessary substantive changes to the journal editor. Send all changes of address to both the journal editor and the APA journal office in Washington. In all correspondence, include the title, author, journal name, and manuscript receipt date.

Proofreading

Before most edited manuscripts are set in type, they are sent to the author from APA. This procedure, which is used when numerous editorial changes occur, allows the author to review the editing and answer all queries. A month or so later, the printer sends the author two sets of proofs (an original to read and a duplicate for his files) and the edited manuscript. These proofs enable an author to catch errors in typesetting; they do not provide an opportunity to rewrite the paper. By reviewing the edited manuscript carefully and then by following the procedure below, authors can help ensure prompt and efficient publication of their manuscripts.

4.26
Reading
Proofs

First, give the printed proofs a literal reading to catch typographical errors. Another person (a copyholder) should read the manuscript aloud slowly while the author reads the proof. Spell out complicated terms letter by letter and call out punctuation to catch all deviations from the manuscript. If there is no copyholder, proofread by glancing from the manuscript to the proof (this method is not as accurate).

Second, carefully read the proofs again, without the manuscript, for sense. This is your chance to be sure you have said what you intended to say. However, it is not the time to rewrite text, only to correct errors or omissions.

Third, check specific points:

- Have you answered any editor's and printer's queries fully?

- Are all numbers in text, tables, and mathematical and statistical copy correct?

- Are tables and figures correct? Do they carry correct captions and numbers?

4.27
Author's
Alterations

Proofreading makes the printed page identical with the manuscript. A change made on the proof for a reason other than agreement with the manuscript is an author's alteration, which an author pays for. Numerous author's alterations may cause delays in publication and often lead to new errors. Extensive additions, deletions, or changes by the author must be approved by the journal editor.

When a change on the proofs is essential, plan the alteration to minimize cost and confusion. Charges are computed according to the number of printed lines affected by a change. Therefore, the cost to change or add words at the end of a paragraph is comparatively small. If a change near the beginning of a paragraph is necessary, count the number of characters and spaces to be removed and make an insertion that will use as nearly as possible the same number of characters and spaces to avoid resetting an entire paragraph. Type or print all changes clearly in the margin of the proof or, if they are long, on a separate sheet attached to the proof. Indicate clearly on the proof where the correction is to be inserted.

Any change in a figure means that a plate must be remade; the figure must be completely redrawn and a new copy submitted.

<table>
<tr><td>4.28
Marking
Proofs</td><td>Make all marks in black pencil only (never ink or colored pencils). Mark all corrections on the proofs; never alter the manuscript when correcting proofs. Because the original proofs are used by the printer, mark neatly, using conventional proofreader's marks (see the inside front cover of this Manual. When an error is found, make two marks, one in the text in the exact plce where the correction is to be made and one in the margin directly opposite the error showing what is to be dofne. For more than ① correction in asingle line, mark the corrections from left to right in the nearest margin and separate them by a slanted line (/) for clarity. do not try to squeeze corrections between the printed lines. Do not write special instructions or questions on the proofs, but include them in an accompanying letter</td></tr>
</table>

Make all marks in **black pencil only** (never ink or colored pencils). Mark all corrections on the proofs; never alter the manuscript when correcting proofs. Because the original proofs are used by the printer, mark neatly, using conventional proofreader's marks (see the inside front cover of this Manual). When an error is found, make two marks, one in the text in the exact place where the correction is to be made and one in the margin directly opposite the error showing what is to be done. For more than one correction in a single line, mark the corrections from left to right in the nearest margin and separate them by a slanted line (/) for clarity. Do not try to squeeze corrections between the printed lines. Do not write special instructions or questions on the proofs, but include them in an accompanying letter.

<table>
<tr><td>4.29
Returning
Proofs and
Manuscript</td><td>Transfer all corrections to the duplicate proofs and retain them for reference. Mail the original proofs and the manuscript within 48 hours to the APA, in care of the particular journal, 1200 17th Street, N.W., Washington, D.C. 20036. If proofs are not returned promptly, publication may be delayed.</td></tr>
</table>

Sample Paper

This sample paper was prepared especially for the *Publication Manual* in order to illustrate some applications of APA style in typed form. It did not go through the APA publication process for consideration of content; it is intended only as an example of a properly typed manuscript. Numbers refer to sections in the Manual.

Covert Rehearsal as a Treatment for Test Anxiety

and an Adjunct to College Counseling

William L. Mikulas

University of West Florida

Running head: Covert Rehearsal as Treatment for Test Anxiety

Abstract

...vert rehearsal a person imagines himself performing, in gradual
..., desired or undesired behaviors and experiencing the appropriate
...quences. In the first of two experiments covert rehearsal de-
... test anxiety and improved grade point averages among college
...ts. Both effects were statistically significant. The second ex-
...nt showed that covert rehearsal was a useful adjunct to college
...ling for a wide range of behaviors. The effect was statistically
...icant when students rated themselves; the direction of the effect
...e same when counselors rated students, but the change was not
...tically significant.

Covert Rehearsal as a Treatment for Test Anxiety

and an Adjunct to College Counseling

Psychologists have developed various approaches to therapeutic change, most involving one-to-one relationships between practitioner and client. However, for many people these therapies are unavailable, undesirable, or too expensive. So these people have often turned to popularized self-help techniques. Surveys of self-help literature (see Klausner, 1965) show that many programs center around the idea that positively and realistically imagined change in the desired direction is the key to actual change.

An example of a self-help approach is discussed in Maltz's (1960) book on "psychocybernetics." Maltz assumes that the nervous system cannot tell the difference between an actual experience and one imagined vividly in detail. Hence, by correct imagining, one can change self-images and behavior, including motor skills, social behavior, self-confidence, neuroses, and so forth. The procedure "consists of creative mental picturing, creatively experiencing through your imagination, and the formation of new automatic reaction patterns by 'acting out' and 'acting as if' " (p. 14).

In one form of yoga meditation people improve themselves by visualizing themselves performing desired behaviors. For example, to help develop courage:

4.13

4.14

4.5

4.15

4.12

4.12

4.16

called covert rehearsal, which is similar to popularized self-
imagination approaches. In this procedure the person imagines himself performing the desired or undesired behaviors in gradual steps
and experiencing the appropriate consequences. Covert rehearsal was
tested on two groups of people, the first with the specific problem
of test anxiety and the second with more general problems. It was
predicted that people who were taught covert rehearsal techniques
would show improvement on the specific problem, whether judged by
themselves or by teachers or by counselors.

Experiment 1

Method

    Subjects. Subjects were drawn from 78 introductory psychology
student volunteers who reported a desire to reduce test anxiety. All
volunteers were administered the Suinn Test Anxiety Behavior Scale
(STABS) (Suinn, 1969). The 50 students with the highest anxiety scores
were randomly assigned to experimental and control groups.

    Covert rehearsal handout. The covert rehearsal procedure was
described in a written handout[1] with three sections: (a) First, the
student was told how to identify and list those specific situations
that elicited test anxiety, based on the behavioral items he had
marked on the STABS. (b) He was then taught how to list sequences of
behaviors leading to each anxiety situation. (c) Finally the student
was instructed how to imagine himself realistically and slowly going
through each sequence of behaviors. He was to imagine pleasant things
happening as a result of each step in the sequence. If at any time he

First of all, then, make some pictures of concrete acts
of kindness or courage. . . . [T]o build this courage into y
own character, go over the pictures again, but this time
step up onto the stage and take the place of the hero depict
there, and feel yourself acting the part. (Wood, 1973, pp.

    These self-imagination approaches may be valid, although pro
ably not for the reasons often given or to the extent often promi
Images of stimuli may lead to responses similar to those produced
external stimuli (King, 1973). We can call up different images t
produce various emotions. Wolpe (1958) has shown that desensitiz
to anxiety associated with imagined scenes readily generalizes to
real-life stimuli. Similarly, Cautela has devised covert procedu
reported to reduce the probability of undesired behaviors. In co
sensitization (Cautela, 1967) the person imagines something avers
associated with the undesired behavior, whereas in covert extinction
(Cautela, 1971) the person imagines the undesired behavior occurring
with no reinforcement. In covert reinforcement (Cautela, 1970)
the person imagines a graduated series of approach responses to a feared
situation, with each step followed by imagined reinforcement. The
whole area of modeling (cf. Bandura, 1969) suggests that covert or
imagined processes guide later behavior. Kazdin (in press) reduced
avoidance responses to snakes with covert modeling (Cautela, Note 1)
where the person imagined models approaching snakes.

    These various covert procedures overlap considerably. There-
fore, in this study they were condensed into a single procedure

3.62

3.4

4.11

started to feel anxious, he was to stop imagining, relax, and start
again a step or two back in the sequence. Each student was told to
practice covert rehearsal at least 30 minutes a day.

    Procedure. As a group the 25 experimental subjects met once for
a half hour to hear the rationale for the procedure. They were given
the covert rehearsal handout and instructed to use it by themselves.
The control subjects met as a group with a discussion leader 1 hour
a week for 5 weeks. Discussion centered on why the students felt
anxious in various situations, particularly in those they had marked
on the STABS.

    Eight weeks after the original assessment all subjects still in
school (24 experimental and 23 control) were readministered the STABS.
In addition, the grade point average (GPA) for each student for the
semester following the experiment was compared with that for the semester
preceding the experiment.

Results

    For each measure--anxiety score and GPA--a subject was considered
to have shown no change if his posttest score fell between ±1 standard
error of his pretest score.

    Test anxiety. As predicted, experimental subjects show a de-
crease in anxiety scores more frequently than control subjects. In
Table 1 are frequencies and chi-square values. Mean pre- and posttest
scores for experimental subjects are 168.64 and 118.79. Comparable
scores for control subjects are 169.36 and 151.51.

4.20

_____

Insert Table 1 about here
_____

3.14

3.21

Grade point average. Experimental subjects show an increase in GPA more frequently than control subjects. See Table 1 for frequencies and chi-square values. Mean GPA values in the semesters preceding and following the experiment are, respectively, 2.41 and 2.89 for the experimental group and 2.33 and 2.56 for the control group.

Experiment 2

Method

Subjects. The subjects were 40 college students who had sought help at the university counseling center. One of the three counselors had seen each student at least twice and had determined that the student required treatment. The students were randomly assigned to experimental and control groups.

Covert rehearsal handout. Although this handout was similar to the material for Experiment 1, the content was more general: (a) First, each student was taught how to specify desired and undesired behaviors and the particular situations in which they occur. (b) Next, he learned to list chains of behaviors leading to each desired or undesired behavior. (c) Finally, with desired behaviors the student learned to realistically imagine himself going through each sequence of behaviors with pleasant events at each step. If he felt anxious, he was to stop imagining, relax, and go back one or two steps. In the

undesired behaviors the student was to imagine the sequence to the undesired behavior and an unpleasant result following ent to perform the undesired behavior.

ocedure. All subjects continued to see their assigned counselors rapy. In addition, I saw the 20 experimental subjects indi-y and gave them the covert rehearsal handout plus instructions ionale for its use. I also saw the control subjects individually, e them Maltz's (1960) Psychocybernetics to read and follow. tions to counselors and students prevented the counselors from to which group any student belonged. After 3, 6, and 9 weeks, udent and his counselor independently rated improvement, using lowing scale: 0 = no improvement or a decline, 1 = slight im-nt, 2 = moderate improvement, 3 = substantial improvement, and 4 = dramatic improvement. Also at 9 weeks I interviewed all students about their use of their particular program.

Results

In Figure 1 are the mean self-ratings of the students at the three time intervals. In Table 2 is a summary of a 2 x 3 (Groups x Time) mixed-design analysis of variance on the data. Neither main effect is significant. However, the Group x Time interaction is significant at the .05 level. Post hoc comparisons of the group differences at 3 and 9 weeks show that the control group's mean self-ratings at 3 weeks are significantly higher than those of the experimental group, t (38) = -2.22, $p < .05$. At 9 weeks the experimental group's mean

self-ratings are higher than those of the control group, t (38) = 3.77, $p < .001$.

_____

Insert Figure 1 and Table 2 about here
_____

In Figure 1 and Table 2 are comparable data and analyses for the mean ratings of the students by counselors. The data show the same crossover effect; however, no effect is statistically significant.

Discussion

In the first experiment, in which covert rehearsal effectively decreased test anxiety, the greatest change was found in the STABS measure. Although STABS items were used in covert rehearsal, simple exposure to the items probably does not account for all of the results, as the control group also spent time with these items. Reports from the discussion leader suggest that the control subjects may have spent more time with these items than did the experimental subjects, who generally dealt with the items only at the end of each imagined behavior sequence. Generality of the effects of covert rehearsal is shown in the improved grade point averages for the experimental subjects. This effect was not large, but test anxiety is just one variable affecting GPA. Most students anxious about tests would probably also profit from counseling in study and exam-taking procedures (Allen, 1972).

In the second experiment covert rehearsal was an effective adjunct to counseling. Interviews revealed that subjects used covert rehearsal for a wide range of problems, such as test anxiety, fear of public speaking, fear of flying, and interpersonal anxiety. The procedure was

3.77

3.14

3.66

3.51

self-control (cf. Thoresen & Mahoney, 1974), as well as studies showing that other covert procedures, such as desensitization (Clark,
1973; Marshall, Note 2), can be self-administered. Psychologists need
to develop more self-control material to reduce the time, expense, and
occasionally the necessity for other therapeutic approaches.

Finally, there is the question, Why does covert rehearsal work?
Additional research could separate the subtle interactions of operant
and respondent variables. From the operant view, imagining a sequence
ps may be successive approximation; from the respondent view, it
moving through a hierarchy as a way to control the strength of the
ed response. In operant conditioning, imagining pleasant scenes
with the behavior can provide reinforcement, as in covert rein-
ent (Cautela, 1970). In addition (or alternatively), it can
e incentive to imagine and extinguish anxiety. From a respondent
ation, imagining pleasant scenes provides positive responses for
rconditioning (Wolpe, 1958). Similarly, imagining something aversive
operant punishment or respondent counterconditioning or both.
modeling may have an effect independent of operant and respondent
les.
owever it works, covert rehearsal is a useful change procedure
ombines the approaches of some well-established techniques into
ess more systematic than many popularized self-help methods.

4.6

also used to rehearse assertive or outgoing behaviors and ways of acting in specific social situations.

At first the control subjects reported more change than the experimental subjects, an effect that later reversed. Interviews with
the subjects suggest that at first the control subjects were excited by
the Maltz book. They had great expectations, which they later felt
were not fulfilled. The experimental subjects, on the other hand, had
some early reservations about the simplicity of the covert rehearsal
procedure but were later pleased when it apparently worked.

The counselors generally perceived less change in the students
than the students found in themselves. Interviews with the counselors
reveal that at the 3-week point the counselors were conservative in
their estimates, feeling that little therapeutic change can be accom-
plished in such a short time. At 9 weeks they allowed for *moderate* change,
but their ratings were tempered by their counseling theories. The
counselors seemed to judge improvement by criteria somewhat different
from the specific behavioral changes that pleased the students, altho
the counselors were probably also influenced by the students' feeling
of improvement.

Although this experiment did not differentiate the relative importance of counseling, covert rehearsal, or their interaction,
future research could delineate those situations in which covert rehe
is best used alone or coupled with other approaches.

The fact that covert rehearsal was successfully learned from a
written handout supports the mushrooming literature on behavioral

Reference Notes

1. Cautela, J. R. Covert modeling. Paper presented at the meeting
   of the Association for the Advancement of Behavior Therapy,
   Washington, D.C., September 1971.

2. Marshall, R. C. S. Personal communication, February 1972.

3.61
4.17

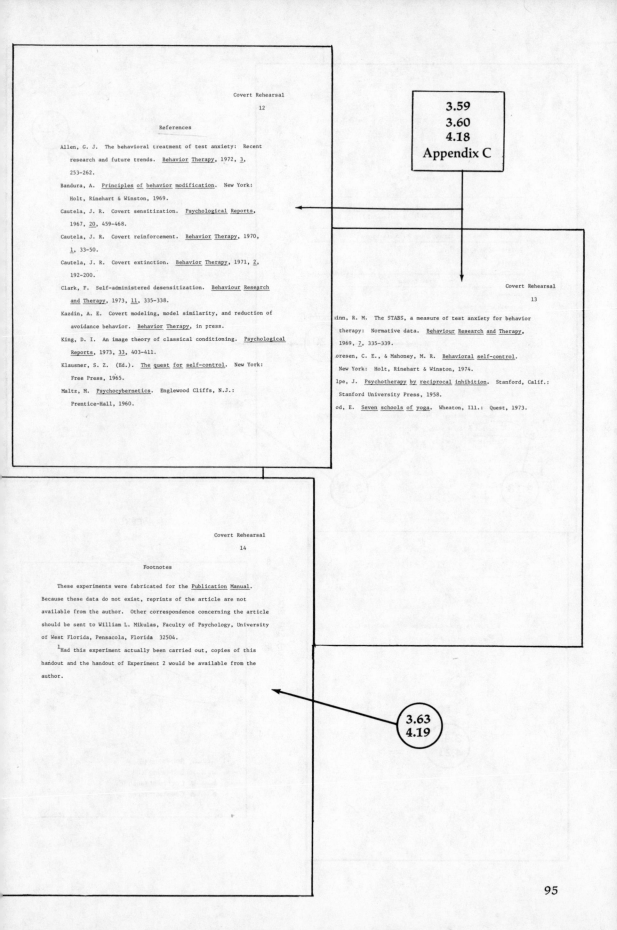

Covert Rehearsal

12

References

Allen, G. J. The behavioral treatment of test anxiety: Recent
   research and future trends. Behavior Therapy, 1972, 3,
   253-262.

Bandura, A. Principles of behavior modification. New York:
   Holt, Rinehart & Winston, 1969.

Cautela, J. R. Covert sensitization. Psychological Reports,
   1967, 20, 459-468.

Cautela, J. R. Covert reinforcement. Behavior Therapy, 1970,
   1, 33-50.

Cautela, J. R. Covert extinction. Behavior Therapy, 1971, 2,
   192-200.

Clark, F. Self-administered desensitization. Behaviour Research
   and Therapy, 1973, 11, 335-338.

Kazdin, A. E. Covert modeling, model similarity, and reduction of
   avoidance behavior. Behavior Therapy, in press.

King, D. I. An image theory of classical conditioning. Psychological
   Reports, 1973, 33, 403-411.

Klausner, S. Z. (Ed.). The quest for self-control. New York:
   Free Press, 1965.

Maltz, M. Psychocybernetics. Englewood Cliffs, N.J.:
   Prentice-Hall, 1960.

3.59
3.60
4.18
Appendix C

Covert Rehearsal

13

...inn, R. M. The STABS, a measure of test anxiety for behavior
   therapy: Normative data. Behaviour Research and Therapy,
   1969, 7, 335-339.

...oresen, C. E., & Mahoney, M. R. Behavioral self-control.
   New York: Holt, Rinehart & Winston, 1974.

...lpe, J. Psychotherapy by reciprocal inhibition. Stanford, Calif.:
   Stanford University Press, 1958.

...od, E. Seven schools of yoga. Wheaton, Ill.: Quest, 1973.

Covert Rehearsal

14

Footnotes

   These experiments were fabricated for the Publication Manual.
Because these data do not exist, reprints of the article are not
available from the author. Other correspondence concerning the article
should be sent to William L. Mikulas, Faculty of Psychology, University
of West Florida, Pensacola, Florida 32504.

   [1]Had this experiment actually been carried out, copies of this
handout and the handout of Experiment 2 would be available from the
author.

3.63
4.19

Table 1

Frequency Data:

Experiment 1

Change score[a]	Group	
	Experimental	Control
Suinn Test Anxiety Behavior Scale scores[b]		
Increase or no change	4	12
Decrease	20	11
Grade point average[c]		
Increase	17	8
Decrease or no change	7	15

[a]No change = posttest score was between ± 1 $\underline{SE}$ of pretest score.

[b]Corrected $\chi^2_{(1)} = 5.10$, $\underline{p} < .025$.

[c]Corrected $\chi^2_{(1)} = 4.76$, $\underline{p} < .05$.

(chi)

3.18

3.33

4.20

Table 2

Analyses of Variance:

Experiment 2

3.12

	Source	df	MS	F
...ater				
...dent	Group (G)	1	2.70	1.18
	Error_b	38	2.27	
	Week (T)	2	.63	1.08
	G x T	2	2.93	5.06*
	Error_w	76	.58	
...nselor	Group (G)	1	3.02	1.53
	Error_b	38	1.97	
	Week (T)	2	2.74	2.06
	G x T	2	3.83	2.88
	Error_w	76	1.33	

*$\underline{p} < .01$.

Figure Caption

Figure 1. Mean ratings of improvement by subjects and by counselors (E = experimental; C = control).

3.43
4.21

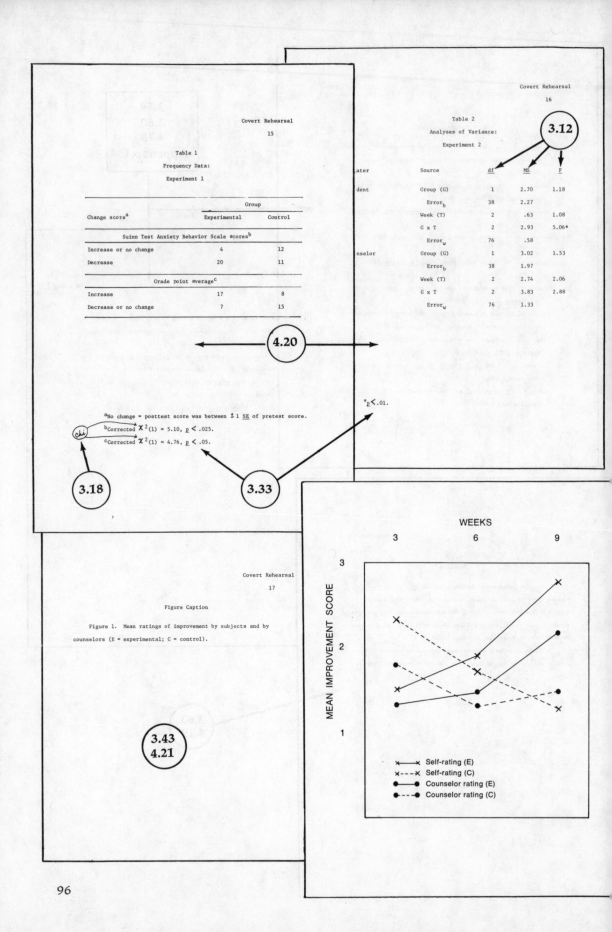

WEEKS

Self-rating (E)
Self-rating (C)
Counselor rating (E)
Counselor rating (C)

5 The Journals of the American Psychological Association

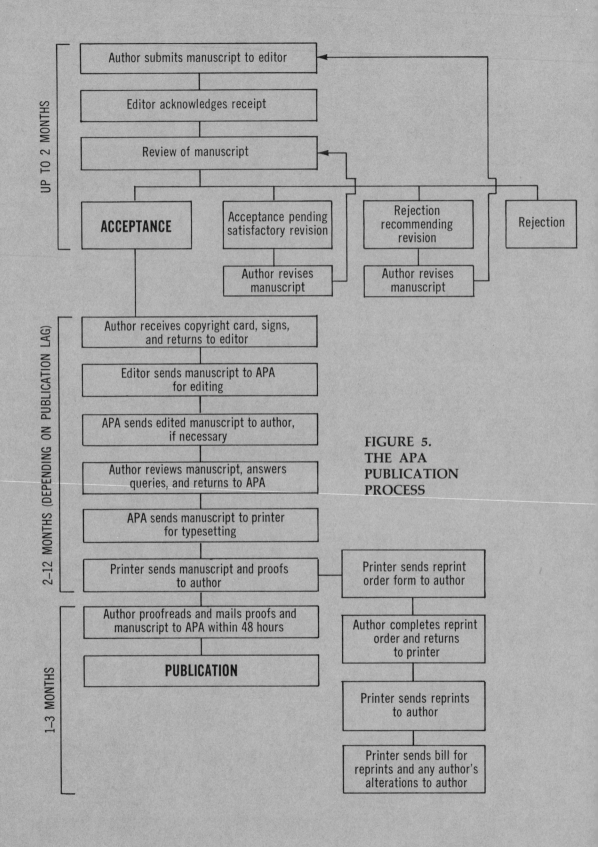

FIGURE 5.
THE APA
PUBLICATION
PROCESS

5 The Journals of the American Psychological Association

The American Psychological Association, founded in 1892 and incorporated in 1925, is the major psychological organization in the United States. With more than 36,000 members in 1974, it includes most of the qualified psychologists in the country.

The purpose of the APA is to advance psychology as a science and as a means of promoting human welfare by encouraging psychology in all its branches in the broadest and most liberal manner. To this end, the APA promotes research and improved research methods and conditions. Through high standards of ethical conduct, education, and achievement, the Association supports continual improvement in the qualifications and competence of psychologists. It disseminates psychological knowledge through meetings, Psychological Abstracts Information Services, and the publication of books and journals.

The Publication Process

Policies and practices for APA journals are established by formal actions of APA's governing bodies and through informal consensus and tradition. The general policies are stated in the Association's Bylaws and Rules of Council; specific ones are enacted by the Publications and Communications Board and the Council of Editors. The policies are implemented by editors, authors, and APA staff concerned with the operation of the journals. Authors should review policies described here for general orientation and should note instructions published in each issue of the journals of interest.

5.1 Policies Governing All Journals

Although an editor's selection of manuscripts determines the quality of a journal from issue to issue, the major policies described below form the framework for editorial decisions for all APA journals. These policies deal with the number of pages a journal publishes, the time between submission and publication of articles, selection of journal editors, and breadth of coverage in the field of psychology.

Page allocation. The Publications and Communications Board limits the number of pages each journal prints each year. In allocating pages, the Board considers the number of manuscripts submitted to a journal, its publication lag, its rejection rate, the availability of other publication outlets, and the provable loss to psychology that might result from delay or rejection of certain material. Each editor is obligated to keep his or her journal within its page allocation and to prevent publication lag from becoming unduly long.

Publication lag. The interval between the receipt of an accepted article and its appearance in print is the publication lag. Each editor aims for a lag of 12 months or less. A large backlog of accepted articles, the time taken for review and revision, and production time contribute to publication lag. APA editors attempt to keep publication lag within bounds by:

- insisting on the greatest brevity possible for adequate presentation of the material
- publishing long manuscripts that integrate several studies instead of shorter articles in a series
- increasing the rate of rejection by establishing more stringent standards of acceptability.

Editorial responsibilities. Journal editors are members of APA who have attained recognition in a special area of psychology. They are appointed by the Publications and Communications Board; they in turn appoint associate editors and reviewers.

The *Editor* of each journal is responsible for all editorial decisions within the policies and rules of procedure established by APA.

The *Associate Editor* of a journal assists the editor in the conduct of the journal, usually with responsibility for specific content within the field of the journal or for a share of the manuscripts received by the editor. An associate editor may act for the editor in all stages of consideration of a manuscript. He may, subject to the editor's review, communicate with the author regarding acceptance, rejection, or required revision.

Consulting Editors, Advisory Editors, or *Issue Consultants* are invited to review manuscripts and make recommendations to editors concerning revision, rejection, or acceptance. These reviewers do not write directly to authors but may draft statements for the editor to use in such correspondence.

The *Managing Editor, Executive Editor,* and *Technical Editors* are employees of the APA Central Office. They are concerned with the management, copy editing, production, and promotion of APA journals.

Journal coverage. Journals are established or discontinued by APA according to its assessment of publication outlets for major areas of psychology and according to changes in areas of journal coverage.

**5.2
Editorial
Practices**

Selection of manuscripts. A manuscript is judged by three main criteria:

- It must make a significant contribution to an area of psychology appropriate to the journal to which it is submitted.

- It must convey its message clearly and as briefly as its content permits.

- It must be in a form that maintains the journal's integrity of style.

Manuscripts that do not meet the first requirement are rejected. Those that do not fully meet the second requirement but are otherwise considered acceptable are returned to the author for revision. Those that do not meet the third requirement may be returned for revision prior to editorial consideration.

APA editors encourage the publication of research that integrates several studies and considers broad implications of results. Authors intending to prepare a series of articles should correspond with the editor concerning the appropriateness of a series. If the manuscripts are already prepared, the author should submit all of them at the same time to the editor, who can then decide whether to accept them separately or to request the author to combine them as a long article or a monograph.

Acknowledgment of receipt and notification of decision. Editors will write a letter of acknowledgment upon receipt of a manuscript and will notify the author of rejection, acceptance, or reason for delay within 2 months. If a manuscript is rejected, one copy becomes the property of the journal and other copies are returned to the author.

Use of unpublished manuscripts. An author is protected by common law against unauthorized use of his unpublished work; therefore, an unpublished manuscript is considered a privileged document. Editors and reviewers may not circulate, quote, cite, or refer in writing or orally to an unpublished work, nor may they use any information in the work to advance their own work without the author's consent.

Procedures in editorial review. Upon receiving a manuscript, the editor either reviews it or sends it to an associate editor or to a reviewer. Where practical, editors employ procedures at the review stage so that authorship is anonymous. (See Table 15 for journals using blind review.)

A reviewer evaluates the manuscript for appropriateness and quality. The editor considers the reviews and informs the author of the decision, which may be (a) outright acceptance; (b) an indication of acceptance if the manuscript can be revised according to specific suggestions; (c) rejection recommending revision, in which case the manuscript is treated as a new manuscript if resubmitted (rejection without prejudice); or (d) outright rejection (see Figure 5). The period for review varies, depending on the nature of the manuscript and on the number of manuscripts in the review process.

Editors do not undertake the major editorial revision of manuscripts being considered for publication. Authors are expected to follow editors' detailed recommendations for (a) revision, (b) condensation, or (c) correction and retyping in order to conform with style specified by this Manual. Should editors wish to undertake major changes themselves, they will consult the author.

Date of receipt of manuscripts. The date of receipt of an accepted manuscript appears with the printed article. This date is ordinarily the date the manuscript is first received in reviewable form, even though an author may later revise the manuscript upon the editor's request. However, if the author fails to meet the editor's deadline for revision, the date on which the *revised* manuscript is received is considered the date of receipt.

The *American Psychologist, Contemporary Psychology,* and *Professional Psychology* do not publish receipt dates.

Order of publication. Most APA journals publish articles in the order of their receipt, but because publication by order of receipt is not always practical or possible, editors may make these exceptions:

- advance or delay an article for the purpose of assembling issues of related topics

- advance an article for a reason they consider legitimate, such as timeliness of brief articles of comment and rejoinder or, more rarely, importance of material

- advance or delay an article in the interest of holding an issue to the most economical number of pages determined by printing requirements.

The *American Psychologist* is exempt from the rule concerning order of publication because it adapts its publication schedule to the requirements of official APA documents and reports and to articles whose value depends on timeliness.

APA has discontinued the policy of allowing authors to secure early publication upon payment of a fee.

**5.3
Author
Requirements**

Preparation of manuscripts. Authors must prepare their manuscripts to conform to the content and style requirements of the current *Publication Manual*. If the manuscript is to be blind reviewed, the author is responsible for preparing the manuscript to conceal his or her identity. (See Table 15 for journals using blind review and section 4.13 for instructions on preparation.)

Submission of manuscripts. Any person may submit a manuscript to an APA journal. Authors are not required to be APA members, nor do they need to be sponsored by a member. Authors usually submit manuscripts on their own initiative, but occasionally an editor may invite an author to submit an article. In no instance are authors paid for their articles.

Multiple submissions. An author must not submit the same manuscript for simultaneous consideration by two or more journals. If a manuscript is rejected by one journal, an author may then submit it to another journal.

Duplicate publication. An author must not submit a manuscript published in whole or in substantial part in another journal or published work. Exceptions may be made for previous publication (a) in a periodical with limited circulation or availability (e.g., a government agency report) or (b) in a summarized form (e.g., the APA *Convention Proceedings*). In either case, an author must inform the editor of the previous publication.

Authorship. Authorship is reserved to those who make major scientific contributions to the research. (See the APA "Ethical Standards of Psychologists," Principle 17: Publication Credit.)

Authors are responsible for the factual accuracy of their contributions. The Association and the editors of its journals assume no responsibility for the statements and opinions advanced by contributors to APA journals. In addition, authors are responsible for providing proof of permission to use previously copyrighted material.

Copyright waiver. Once an article is accepted, an author assigns literary rights on the published article to APA. (An article will not be published until the editor receives the copyright waiver card.) The copyright for APA journal articles is owned by the Association for 28 years and then it reverts to public domain.

Changes in manuscripts. Both journal editors and copy editors introduce changes to achieve consistency with APA style, to correct errors of form, or to improve details of expression. If the number of changes are numerous, authors will be given an opportunity to review their edited manuscripts before they are set in type. During this review, editing should not be changed unless it affects meaning. The author should answer all queries on the manuscript and take this opportunity to correct errors and omissions so that he can avoid author alteration charges at the later proof stage. Any significant substantive changes at this stage must be reviewed by the journal editor.

Proofreading. When the author receives the printed proofs of his article, he is responsible for carefully proofreading them and mailing them with the edited manuscript to APA within 48 hours. If the manuscript and proofs are not returned promptly, publication may be delayed.

Changes on printed proofs should be limited to correcting printer's errors, and updating reference citations or inserting address changes not available when the manuscript went to the printer. Changes that reflect preferences in wording should not be made at this time. Any significant substantive changes at this stage, as at the manuscript review stage, must be approved by the journal editor.

Authors do not pay for changes made in the manuscript before it is set in type. Authors are charged the cost of any alterations they make later on printed proofs when such alterations result from their own errors, omissions, or failure to review the edited manuscript when requested. Authors do not pay for correcting errors made by the printer. At 1974 prices, the charge by printers for corrections on proofs is over $1 for each line affected by the change; authors should bear in mind that even the addition of a comma costs money. The 1974 rate is subject to increase.

Reprints. Authors may order reprints when the proofs are returned to the printer. Rates vary according to the length of the article and the number of copies ordered. Reprints are usually delivered 6–8 weeks after publication of the article.

Authors are permitted to reproduce their articles for personal use without obtaining permission from APA as long as the material incorporates the copyright notice that appears on the original publication. Sale of such copies violates APA policy.

Copyright. APA owns the copyright on material published in its journals. As noted above, authors may reproduce their own material for personal use; if they use their own material commercially, they must secure prior written permission from APA. Anyone else wishing to reproduce, in whole or in part, APA-copyrighted materials for commercial purposes must pay a fee to APA and apply for written permission from the Association. APA usually requests that applicants secure the concurrence of the author whose material is being reprinted.

The Journals

Since 1925, APA has published scientific journals, acquiring some by gift, purchase, or merger and creating others. As the list of journals has grown, the Association has adapted its journal editorial policies to fit the needs occasioned by the growth of psychology as a science and a profession.

The present coverage of the journals is described in the following editorial statements. These statements should help a prospective author differentiate among the journals and choose an appropriate one for his manuscript. Authors should also examine current issues of the journals to become familiar with each journal's specific content and any special instructions to authors. (See also Table 15 for additional editorial information.)

The **American Psychologist** is the official journal of the American Psychological Association and, as such, contains archival documents. It also publishes articles on current issues in psychology as well as empirical, theoretical, and practical articles on broad aspects of psychology.

Contemporary Psychology contains critical reviews of books, films, tapes, and other media relevant to psychology. Material reviewed is intended to present a cross section of psychological literature suitable for a broad readership. All reviews are written by invitation, but readers may submit brief letters about published reviews.

Developmental Psychology publishes articles that significantly advance knowledge about growth and development. The Journal is primarily intended for reports of empirical research in which the developmental implications are clear and convincing. Any variable or set of variables that helps to promote understanding of psychological processes and their development within the life span is appropriate.

The **Journal of Abnormal Psychology** publishes articles on basic research and theory in the broad field of abnormal behavior, its determinants, and its correlates. The following general topics fall within its area of major focus: (a) psychopathology—its etiology, development, symptomatology, and course; (b) normal processes in abnormal individuals; (c) pathological or atypical features of the behavior of normal persons; (d) experimental studies, with human or animal subjects, relating to disordered emotional behavior or pathology; (e) social or group effects on pathological processes; and (f) tests of hypotheses from psychoanalytic or other psychological theories that relate to abnormal behavior. Thus, case histories, experiments on hypnosis, theoretical papers of scholarly substance on deviant personality and emotional abnormality, studies of patient populations, and analyses of abnormal behavior and motivation in terms of modern behavior theories would all fall within the boundaries of the Journal's interests. Each article should represent an addition to knowledge and understanding of abnormal behavior either in its etiology, description, or change. In order to improve the use of journal resources, it has been agreed by the two editors concerned that the *Journal of Abnormal Psychology* will no longer consider articles dealing with the diagnosis or treatment of abnormal behavior, and the *Journal of Consulting and Clinical Psychology* will no longer consider manuscripts dealing with the etiology or descriptive pathology of abnormal behavior. Articles that appear to have a significant contribution to both of these broad areas may be sent to either journal for editorial decision.

The **Journal of Applied Psychology** is devoted primarily to original investigations that contribute new knowledge and understanding to any field of applied psychology except clinical psychology. The Journal considers quantitative investigations of interest to psychologists doing research or working in such settings as universities, industry, government, urban affairs, police and correctional systems, health and educational institutions, transportation and defense systems, and consumer affairs. A theoretical or review article may be accepted if it represents a special contribution to an applied field.

The **Journal of Comparative and Physiological Psychology** publishes research reports that make a substantial and significant contribution to the literature. Preference is given to experimental reports that elucidate physiological mechanisms of behavior or truly comparative aspects of behavior. Authors should seriously weigh whether their paper is chiefly directed toward clarification of physiological, anatomical, or chemical mechanisms of behavior (for the physiological emphasis of the Journal) or biological mechanisms, whether genetic, maturational, or experiential, of species-typical behavior (for the comparative emphasis of the Journal). Experimental papers oriented toward behavior theory regardless of type of subject should be sent to the appropriate section of the *Journal of Experimental Psychology.*

The **Journal of Consulting and Clinical Psychology** publishes original contributions on the following topics: (a) the development, validity, and use of techniques of diagnosis and treatment in disordered behavior; (b) studies of populations of clinical interest, such as hospital, prison, rehabilitation, geriatric, and similar samples; (c) cross-cultural and demographic studies of interest for the behavior disorders; (d) studies of personality and of its assessment and development where these have a clear bearing on problems of consulting and clinical psychology; or (e) case studies pertinent to the preceding topics. In order to improve the use of journal resources, it has been agreed by the two editors concerned that the *Journal of Consulting and Clinical Psychology* will no longer consider manuscripts dealing with the etiology or descriptive pathology of abnormal behavior, and the *Journal of Abnormal Psychology* will no longer consider articles dealing with the diagnosis or treatment of abnormal behavior. Articles that appear to have a significant contribution to both of these broad areas may be sent to either journal for editorial decision. Papers of a theoretical nature will also be considered within the space limitations that prevail for the Journal generally.

The **Journal of Counseling Psychology** publishes articles on theory, research, and practice concerning counseling and related activities of counselors and personnel workers. Particular attention is given to articles dealing with the developmental aspects of counseling, as well as to diagnostic, group, remedial, and therapeutic approaches. The Journal occasionally includes topical reviews of research and other systematic surveys and also measurement and research methodology studies directly related to counseling. Reviews of tests used by counselors and basic theoretical contributions are published periodically. The Journal is designed to be of interest to psychologists and counselors in schools, colleges, and universities; public and private agencies; business and industry; and religious and military agencies.

The **Journal of Educational Psychology** publishes original investigations and theoretical papers dealing with learning and cognition, especially as they relate to problems of instruction, and with the psychological development, relationships, and adjustment of the individual. Preference is given to studies of the more complex types of behavior, especially in or relating to educational settings. Journal articles pertain to all levels of education and to all age groups.

Starting in 1975, the **Journal of Experimental Psychology** appears as four independently edited and distributed sections:

The **Journal of Experimental Psychology: General** publishes articles in any area of experimental psychology when the articles involve a longer, more integrative report leading to an advance in knowledge that is judged to be of interest to the entire community of experimental psychologists. The section will include but not be limited to articles such as those that have appeared as *Journal of Experimental Psychology* monographs and as chapters in contemporary books of "advances." Republication of a limited number of data may be permitted if necessary to make the article complete and definitive.

The **Journal of Experimental Psychology: Human Learning and Memory** publishes experimental studies on fundamental acquisition, retention, and transfer processes in human behavior.

The **Journal of Experimental Psychology: Human Perception and Performance** publishes experimental studies designed to foster understanding of information-processing operations and their relation to experience and performance.

The **Journal of Experimental Psychology: Animal Behavior Processes** publishes experimental studies concerning the basic mechanisms of perception, learning, motivation, and performance, especially as revealed in the behavior of infrahuman animals. The studies should make significant contributions to general behavior theory.

The **Journal of Personality and Social Psychology** publishes original research reports in the areas of social psychology and personality dynamics. The Journal includes articles on the following topics: social motivation; attitudes and attitude change; social interaction; verbal and nonverbal communication processes; group behavior; person perception; conformity and deviation; and personality structure and dynamics. Methodological articles, studies primarily concerned with the development of measuring instruments, replications, and reports of negative results or failures to replicate published work are acceptable if they are judged to make a substantial contribution to knowledge. Low priority is given to papers concerned with personality assessment or the development and validation of assessment instruments. Manuscripts in these latter categories should be brief, not more than nine typewritten pages. The Journal does not include studies of abnormal processes or populations.

Professional Psychology publishes original articles on conceptual and practical issues, including articles on applications of research, standards of practice, interprofessional relations, delivery of services, and innovative approaches to training. The Journal also provides a forum for the exchange of opinions; current bibliographies; and reviews of films, tests, and other materials related to the practice of psychology. The Journal is designed to be of interest not only to psychologists but also to students and the general public who want to learn about the roles and functions of psychologists.

The **Psychological Bulletin** publishes evaluative reviews and interpretations of substantive and methodological issues in the psychological research literature. The Journal reports original research only when it illustrates some methodological problem or issue. Discussions of methodological issues should be aimed at the solution of some particular research problem in psychology, but should be of sufficient breadth to interest a wide readership among psychologists; articles of a more specialized nature can be directed to the various statistical, psychometric, and methodological journals. The *Bulletin* does not publish original theoretical articles; these should be submitted to the *Psychological Review*.

The **Psychological Review** publishes articles that make theoretical contributions to any area of scientific psychology. Preference is given to papers that advance theory rather than review it, and to statements that are specifically theoretical rather than programmatic. Surveys of the literature, problems of method and design, and papers that primarily report empirical findings are ordinarily not appropriate.

Journal-Related Periodicals

Psychological Abstracts publishes nonevaluative abstracts of the world's literature in psychology and related disciplines. In addition to the monthly journal of abstracts, semiannual volume indexes and 3-year cumulative indexes are published. The abstracts are also available on machine-readable tape, which provides the facility for automated search and retrieval services. These services fall into three main categories: PASAR (*PA* Search and Retrieval), for the individual requester; PADAT (*PA* Direct Access Terminal), for searching the *PA* data base on a computer terminal in an individual's facility; and PATELL (*PA* Tape Edition Lease and Licensing), for annual leasing of *PA* machine-readable tapes from 1967 to the present by information centers. All of these services are part of the *Psychological Abstracts* Information Services (PAIS).

The Journal Supplement Abstract Service (JSAS) provides an intermediate publication outlet between informal communication networks and conventional journals. Original materials of all types, formats, lengths, and psychological content are appropriate for submission to the editors. Accepted papers are abstracted in the JSAS **Catalog of Selected Documents in Psychology** along with notation of document length and price per copy. Full-text documents may be ordered in hard copy or microfiche. (See Appendix A, JSAS.)

The **APA Monitor** is a monthly newspaper that publishes news stories of a nonarchival nature about psychology and current APA activities. It also contains news about government and legislative activity relating to psychological issues.

See next page for Table 15:
APA Journal Editors
and Addresses

Table 15: APA Journal Editors and Addresses

Editors and institutional affiliations change. Always check a recent issue of the journal for current editorial address before submitting a manuscript. General queries about journals should be directed to the Executive Editor, Journal Office, APA, 1200 17th Street, N.W., Washington, D.C. 20036.

Information on publication lag, rejection rate, and circulation of each journal is published annually in the *American Psychologist*.

Journal, editorial address, and editor's term	Manuscript copies required	Sections [a]	Blind review	Recent editorial statement
American Psychologist Kenneth B. Little (undesignated term) Executive Officer, APA 1200 17th Street, N.W. Washington, D.C. 20036	3	Articles Archival documents Announcements Calendars Comments	Yes	1965, *20*, 121–122 1970, *25*, 986 1973, *28*, 139
Contemporary Psychology Janet T. Spence (1974–1979) Department of Psychology University of Texas Austin, TX 78712	2	Reviews [b] Brief reviews Letters to editor	No	1972, *17*, 643–645 1974, *19*, 1–2
Developmental Psychology Richard D. Odom (1975–1980) Department of Psychology 134 Wesley Hall Vanderbilt University Nashville, TN 37240	3	Articles Brief reports Monographs	Yes	1970, *2*, 1–4 1971, *4*, 1
Journal of Abnormal Psychology Leonard D. Eron (1973–1979) Department of Psychology Box 4348 University of Illinois at Chicago Circle Chicago, IL 60680	3	Articles Short reports Monographs	No	1974, *83*, 213–214
Journal of Applied Psychology Edwin A. Fleishman (1971–1976) American Institutes for Research 3301 New Mexico Avenue, N.W. Washington, D.C. 20016	3	Articles Short notes Monographs	Yes [c]	1971, *55*, 1–2
Journal of Comparative and Physiological Psychology Garth J. Thomas (1975–1980) Center for Brain Research Medical Center University of Rochester Rochester, NY 14642	3	Articles Monographs	No	1969, *67*, 1–2 *American Psychologist*, 1974, *29*, 65–66

See footnotes at end of table, p. 112.

Table 15—Continued

Journal, editorial address, and editor's term	Manuscript copies required	Sections [a]	Blind review	Recent editorial statement
Journal of Consulting and Clinical Psychology Brendan A. Maher (1974–1979) 1120 William James Hall Harvard University 33 Kirkland Street Cambridge, MA 02138	3	Articles Brief reports Monographs	No	1974, 42, 1–3
Journal of Counseling Psychology Ralph F. Berdie (1970–1978) 408 Morrill Hall University of Minnesota Minneapolis, MN 55455	2	Articles Brief reports Test reviews Monographs	Yes	1973, 20(5), un-numbered
Journal of Educational Psychology Joanna Williams (1973–1978) P.O. Box 51 Teachers College Columbia University New York, NY 10027	3	Articles Monographs	Yes	1973, 64(1), un-numbered
Journal of Experimental Psychology: General Gregory A. Kimble (1975–1980) Department of Psychology University of Colorado Boulder, CO 80302	3	Articles Monographs	Yes [c]	*American Psychologist,* 1974, 29, 65–66
Journal of Experimental Psychology: Human Learning and Memory Lyle E. Bourne, Jr. (1975–1980) Department of Psychology University of Colorado Boulder, CO 80302	3	Articles	Yes [c]	*American Psychologist,* 1974, 29, 65–66
Journal of Experimental Psychology: Human Perception and Performance Michael I. Posner (1975–1980) Department of Psychology University of Oregon Eugene, OR 97403	3	Articles	Yes [c]	*American Psychologist,* 1974, 29, 65–66
Journal of Experimental Psychology: Animal Behavior Processes Allan R. Wagner (1975–1980) Department of Psychology Yale University New Haven, CT 06510	3	Articles	Yes [c]	*American Psychologist,* 1974, 29, 65–66
Journal of Personality and Social Psychology John T. Lanzetta (1971–1976) Department of Psychology Dartmouth College Hanover, NH 03755	2	Articles	Yes	1965, 1, 1–2

See footnotes at end of table, p. 112.

Table 15—Continued

Journal, editorial address, and editor's term	Manuscript copies required	Sections [a]	Blind review	Recent editorial statement
Professional Psychology Donald K. Freedheim (1969–1976) Department of Psychology Case Western Reserve University Cleveland, OH 44106	3	Articles Symposia The Forum Departments Editorials	No	1973, 4, 258 *American Psychologist*, 1973, 28, 139
Psychological Bulletin R. J. Herrnstein (1975–1980) William James Hall Harvard University 33 Kirkland Street Cambridge, MA 02138	2	Articles	Yes	1965, 63, 73
Psychological Review George Mandler (1971–1976) Department of Psychology University of California, San Diego La Jolla, CA 92037	3	Articles Monographs Theoretical notes Letters to editor	Yes	1965, 72, 1–2 1971, 78, 1–2

[a] Sections:

Articles are normally 3–20 printed pages.

Short and *brief reports* are usually limited to 3 printed pages and report simple or preliminary experiments, extensions, replications, or summaries. They are usually published sooner than articles, and extended reports are sometimes available from the author. Requirements for length, content, and format appear in each journal.

Monographs usually run at least 20 printed pages and report related studies or a single extensive study. Through 1966 these studies were published by APA in *Psychological Monographs*; from 1967 to 1970 they were separate supplements to each journal; since 1970 they have been bound within each journal.

Other sections (e.g., letters to the editor, test reviews) are described in the appropriate journals.

[b] Reviews for *Contemporary Psychology* are written by invitation only.

[c] Blind review only if requested by author.

6 Bibliography

The bibliography is divided into three sections: The first section, which gives the historical background of the APA *Publication Manual*, lists the predecessors of this edition in chronological order. The second section is an alphabetical listing of all references cited in this Manual. The third section, which is subdivided and annotated for easy use, suggests further reading.

6.1 History of the Publication Manual

Instructions in regard to preparation of manuscript. *Psychological Bulletin*, 1929, *26*, 57–63.

Anderson, J. E., & Valentine, W. L. The preparation of articles for publication in the journals of the American Psychological Association. *Psychological Bulletin*, 1944, *41*, 345–376.

American Psychological Association, Council of Editors. Publication manual of the American Psychological Association. *Psychological Bulletin*, 1952, *49*, 389–449. (Supplement)

American Psychological Association, Council of Editors. *Publication manual of the American Psychological Association* (Rev. ed.). Washington, D.C.: Author, 1957.

American Psychological Association. *Publication manual of the American Psychological Association* (Rev. ed.). Washington, D.C.: Author, 1967.

6.2 References Cited in the Second Edition

American National Standard for the preparation of scientific papers for written or oral presentation (ANSI Z39.16-1972). New York: American National Standards Institute, 1972.

American Psychological Association, Committee on Ethical Standards in Psychological Research. *Ethical principles in the conduct of research with human participants*. Washington, D.C.: Author, 1973.

American Psychological Association, Committee on Precautions and Standards in Animal Experimentation. *Principles for the care and use of animals*. Washington, D.C.: Author, 1971. (Available free on request from the APA Board of Scientific Affairs.)

Bruner, K. F. Of psychological writing: Being some valedictory remarks on style. *Journal of Abnormal and Social Psychology*, 1942, *37*, 52–70.

Ethical standards of psychologists. *American Psychologist*, 1963, *18*, 56–60. (Amended in 1965 and 1972 by the APA Council of Representatives and reprinted in the *Casebook on Ethical Standards of Psychologists*, the *Biographical Directory of the American Psychological Association*, and the *Consolidated Roster for Psychology*, all published by APA. Individual copies also available from APA Publication Sales.)

Maher, B. A. Editorial. *Journal of Consulting and Clinical Psychology*, 1974, *42*, 1–3.

Schlosberg, H. Hints on presenting a paper at an APA convention. *American Psychologist*, 1965, *20*, 606–607.

Skillin, M. E., & Gay, R. M. *Words into type* (3rd ed.). Englewood Cliffs, N.J.: Prentice-Hall, 1974.

A uniform system of citation: Forms of citation and abbreviations (11th ed.). Cambridge, Mass.: Harvard Law Review Association, 1967.

University of Chicago Press. *A manual of style* (12th ed., rev.). Chicago: Author, 1969.

U.S. Government Printing Office. *Style manual* (Rev. ed.). Washington, D.C.: Author, 1973.

Webster's new collegiate dictionary. Springfield, Mass.: Merriam, 1973.

Webster's third new international dictionary of the English language, unabridged. Springfield, Mass.: Merriam, 1971.

6.3 Suggested Reading

General

Skillin, M. E., & Gay, R. M. *Words into type* (3rd ed.). Englewood Cliffs, N.J.: Prentice-Hall, 1974. Detailed guide to the preparation of manuscripts, handling of copy and proofs, copy-editing style, typographical style, grammar and word usage, and typography and illustration.

University of Chicago Press. *A manual of style* (12th ed., rev.). Chicago: Author, 1969. A standard for authors, editors, printers, and proofreaders which provides clear and simple guidelines for preparing and editing copy. Gives attention to the technicalities of preparing copy, such as mathematical material, for scientific publication.

Writing Style

Bernstein, T. M. *Miss Thistlebottom's hobgoblins.* New York: Farrar, Strauss & Giroux, 1971. Subtitled as "the careful writer's guide to the taboos, bugbears, and outmoded rules of English usage."

Boring, E. G. CP speaks . . . . *Contemporary Psychology*, 1957, *2*, 279. An editorial on psychologists and good writing by the first editor of *Contemporary Psychology*.

Harlow, H. F. Fundamental principles for preparing psychology journal articles. *Journal of Comparative and Physiological Psychology*, 1962, *55*, 893–896. An editor's humorous remarks on the content and style of scientific reporting.

Strunk, W., Jr., & White, E. B. *The elements of style* (2nd ed.). New York: Macmillan, 1972. A classic that offers concise, clear advice on achieving good writing style.

Woodford, F. P. Sounder thinking through clearer writing. *Science*, 1967, *156*, 743–745. Suggests that a graduate course on scientific writing can strengthen and clarify scientific thinking.

Mathematics

American Institute of Physics. *Style manual* (2nd ed., rev.). New York: Author, 1970. Includes a detailed section on presenting mathematical expressions, as well as six pages of special characters and signs available in type.

Note: See also chapter 13, "Mathematics in Type," in the University of Chicago Press *Manual of Style.*

Metrication

Page, C. H., & Vigoureux, P. (Eds.). *The International System of Units (SI)* (National Bureau of Standards Special Publication 330). Washington, D.C.: U.S. Government Printing Office, 1972. The approved translation of the French

Le Système International d'Unités. Contains the resolutions and recommendations of the General Conference of Weights and Measures on SI, as well as recommendations for the practical use of SI.

The Royal Society Conference of Editors. Metrication in scientific journals. *American Scientist*, 1968, *56*, 159–164. A reprinting of a pamphlet prepared to promote the adoption of the metric system of units in the scientific and technical journals of the United Kingdom.

Standard metric practice guide (ASTM E380-72). Philadelphia, Pa.: American Society for Testing and Materials, 1972. (Also ANSI Z210.1-1973) Includes sections on SI units and symbols, rules for SI style and usage, rules for conversion and rounding, as well as a 14-page appendix of conversion factors.

Figures

Illustrations for publication and projection (ASA Y15.1-1959). New York: American National Standards Institute, 1959. Explains and illustrates the preparation of legible and effective diagrams and graphs for technical publications or projections.

Typing

Dunford, N. J. *A handbook for technical typists.* New York: Gordon & Breach, 1964. Contains helpful instructions on typing mathematical and other technical material.

Student Papers

Linton, M. *A simplified style manual: For the preparation of journal articles in psychology, social sciences, education, and literature.* New York: Appleton-Century-Crofts, 1972. Expands the recommendations of the 1967 APA *Publication Manual* for student use with examples and annotations.

Turabian, K. L. *A manual for writers of term papers, theses, and dissertations* (4th ed.). Chicago: University of Chicago Press, 1973. Based on the University of Chicago Press *Manual of Style.* Provides style guidelines for the typewritten presentation of formal papers.

APA Publications

Ordering information on all APA publications and information services is available free on request from APA Publication Sales, 1200 17th Street, N.W., Washington, D.C. 20036.

Appendix A: Material Other Than Journal Articles

Although the APA *Publication Manual* is intended primarily as a guide to preparing manuscripts for journal publication, it is also used for preparing theses, dissertations, and student papers; papers for oral presentation; and papers published in abbreviated form. This appendix explains some of the differences between these materials and journal articles.

Theses, Dissertations, and Student Papers

The differences in preparing journal articles and theses, dissertations, or student papers lie in two areas: content and typing. Both are dictated by the purpose of the material, the needs of the reader, and economics. (*Note:* A thesis or dissertation in its original form is not acceptable to APA journals.)

Content

Requirements for the content of student papers may coincide with those for manuscripts submitted for publication. However, the purpose of the paper and the reading audience (professor or committee members) may dictate variations. Students should be aware of the possibility of differences and ascertain special requirements.

Preliminary pages. Introductory material for a thesis or dissertation usually includes a title page, approval page, acknowledgments, table of contents, list of tables and figures, and an abstract.

The maximum length for a dissertation abstract (for submission to *Dissertation Abstracts International*) is 600 words, far longer than the 100–175 words for APA journals. In psychology dissertations, substituting the abstract for the summary has become a common practice, but the decision is usually left to the author and his or her committee. In general, standards for theses and dissertations are similar. Abstracts for student laboratory reports are more often expected to follow APA limits on length.

Introduction. Theses and dissertations may include long introductory sections in which the student demonstrates familiarity with the literature. The decision about length is usually delegated to the department or to the committee chair; thus, requirements vary widely.

Students writing laboratory reports are often permitted to cite material from secondary sources with appropriate referencing; this practice is not encouraged in journal articles, theses, or dissertations.

Method, results, and discussion. The content of these sections in student papers is similar to that of journal articles.

Summary. As noted, the trend is to substitute the abstract for the summary.

References. An occasional exception can be found to the rule that only references cited in the text are included in the reference list. An example is when a committee or department requires evidence that a student is familiar with a broader spectrum of literature than that immediately relevant to his or her research. In such instances, the reference list may be called a bibliography.

Appendixes. Although space and content requirements usually limit the use of appendixes in journal articles, the need for complete documentation often dictates their inclusion in student papers. The following materials are appropriate for an appendix: verbatim instructions to subjects, original scales or questionnaires, and raw data. In addition, subject sign-up sheets or informed consent forms and statistical calculations may be required in appendixes to laboratory reports.

Typing

The typing guidelines that follow may not be applicable to laboratory reports, because in laboratory courses students are often expected to prepare reports in the style required for actual submission to an appropriate journal.

Each university has requirements for the format of theses and dissertations which differ from those in this Manual. The purpose of their requirements is similar to one purpose of this Manual: to obtain uniformity in manuscripts by individuals from a variety of disciplines. *The student should find out whether (or in what respects) the university's thesis–dissertation manual requirements take precedence over those of this Manual.* Generally, university requirements permit departmental variation in certain areas.

As writers apply these guidelines to typing, they should be aware that the typewritten copy is the final copy. Because the manuscript will not be set in type, the appearance of the copy will not be changed to improve readability.

Paper, corrections, copies, and margins. Most requirements for rag content and weight of paper are established to provide durable copies of theses and dissertations for the library. Beyond contributing to appearance, the few permissible correction methods also provide for durability. Some universities still require carbon copies, but many universities now permit photocopies. The left-hand margin must be wide enough for binding, usually 1½ inches (4 cm). The top margin on the first page of a new chapter (section) may be wider than other margins. Typists should observe requirements carefully because some of each margin is trimmed in the binding process.

Chapters. The sections of a research report (Introduction, Method, Results, and Discussion) are frequently regarded as chapters; each begins on a new page. They may or may not include a chapter number.

In APA style, the introduction is not labeled. However, the arrangement of materials in most theses and dissertations may require that the introduction be labeled because no other heading appears on that page.

Figures, tables, and footnotes. Although figures, tables, and footnotes are placed at the end of a manuscript submitted for publication, such material is frequently incorporated at the appropriate point in text in theses and dissertations. This placement is a convenience to readers, particularly when they are reading the manuscript in microform. Short tables may appear on a page with some text. Each long table and each figure are placed on a separate page immediately following the first mention. Figure captions are typed below the figure or, in some cases, on the preceding or facing page. Footnotes to the text are typed at the bottom of the page on which they are referenced.

Pagination. Preliminary pages usually carry lowercase roman numerals. Throughout the manuscript, certain pages may be counted in the numbering sequence without actually carrying a number. The position of numbers on the first pages of chapters or on full-page tables and figures may differ from the position on other pages. Page numbers continue throughout the appendix.

Spacing. Double-spacing is required throughout most of the manuscript. However, when single-spacing would improve readability, it is usually encouraged. Examples of efficient use of single-spacing are: in table titles and headings, in figure captions, in references (but double-spacing *between* references), in footnotes, and in long quotations. Long quotations may also be indented five spaces.

Judicious triple- or quadruple-spacing can improve appearance and readability. Such spacing is appropriate after chapter titles, before major subheadings, before footnotes, and before and after tables in the text.

Material for Oral Presentation

If you are active in research, you probably will have occasion to present a paper at a convention, symposium, workshop, seminar, or other gathering of professional people. Material delivered orally differs from written material in its level of detail, organization, and presentation. Even the best research may sound inferior depending on the speaker and the conditions under which he is speaking. The speaker who prepares himself adequately can strengthen his performance.

The following hints, taken from an article

by Harold Schlosberg in the July 1965 *American Psychologist* (pp. 606–607), may be helpful in preparing a paper for oral presentation:

- Your primary purpose is to communicate clearly under less-than-ideal conditions. Concentrate on getting across only one or two main points.

- Although most people advise against reading a manuscript, have one in front of you for support. Mark it so you can find your place if you break off to elaborate on a point or to show slides. If you use visual materials, stage a trial run to make certain that they can be read and understood from a distance.

- Rehearsal is necessary for a skillful performance. Read the manuscript aloud to test its continuity and phrasing. Read it again, timing it. Hold a dress rehearsal if possible, presenting the paper under conditions similar to the real-life session.

Material Published in Abbreviated Form

In addition to publishing research in its entirety as journal articles, authors may make their research available through these means:

- APA's Journal Supplement Abstract Service (JSAS)

- Brief reports in APA journals

- National Auxiliary Publications Service (NAPS).

JSAS

The Journal Supplement Abstract Service publishes abstracts of accepted manuscripts in the *Catalog of Selected Documents in Psychology*. Interested readers may order the full documents. Guidelines for manuscript preparation, submission, and acceptance are printed in the *Catalog*. JSAS is a publication service developed to

(a) provide ready access to diverse materials unavailable through journals;

(b) make available items of value to a small, specialized audience;

(c) encourage submission of materials not normally considered because they are too bulky for standard publication and uneconomical for large distribution;

(d) increase knowledge about and provide an outlet for materials distributed through informal communications channels that should reach a wider audience and be retrievable through *Psychological Abstracts*.

Brief Reports

Studies of specialized interest or limited importance are published as brief reports in some of the APA journals. The report in the journal, usually one or two pages, summarizes the procedure and results of a study. Usually printed with the report is the address of the author to whom requests for an extended report should be sent. Refer to the appropriate journals for details on preparing brief reports. (See Table 15 for journals that publish brief reports.)

NAPS

The National Auxiliary Publications Service is operated as a service of the American Society for Information Science. Authors may deposit with NAPS any supplementary materials, such as original observations, extensive calculations, or detailed drawings, that cannot be included economically in a printed article or that may be of interest to only a few readers. So that readers may order copies, the printed article carries a footnote indicating that materials are available from NAPS. The author is responsible for depositing the materials with NAPS and including the footnote. This is done at his own expense. Authors should direct all inquiries to:

ASIS/NAPS
c/o Microfiche Publications
305 East 46th Street
New York, NY 10017.

Appendix B: Non-APA Journals Using the APA Publication Manual

Although the *Publication Manual* is intended for authors writing for APA journals, many related journals instruct their authors to prepare their manuscripts according to the APA *Publication Manual*. Some journals may use the entire Manual, and others may use only the reference style.

The following list includes the names of non-APA journals using the Manual at the time this edition went to press. Authors who wish to submit manuscripts to these journals should consult recent issues of the journals for current editorial addresses and special requirements. Additions, deletions, or corrections to the list, as well as comments on the Manual, should be sent to Journal Office, Attention: Publication Manual, APA, 1200 17th Street, N.W., Washington, D.C. 20036. For other psychological journals, refer to the coverage list published in *Psychological Abstracts*.

American Educational Research Journal
American Journal of Community Psychology
American Journal of Mental Deficiency
American Journal of Psychology
Animal Learning & Behavior

Behavior Research Methods & Instrumentation
Behavior Therapy
Behavioral and Social Science Teacher
Bulletin of the Psychonomic Society

Canadian Journal of Behavioural Science
Canadian Journal of Psychology
Canadian Psychologist
Child Care Quarterly
Child Development
Clinical Social Work Journal
Cognitive Psychology
Community Mental Health Journal
Counseling and Values
Counselor Education and Supervision

Elementary School Guidance and Counseling

International Journal of Clinical and Experimental Hypnosis
International Journal of Group Tensions
International Review of Applied Psychology

Journal of Abnormal Child Psychology
Journal of Applied Behavior Analysis
Journal of Applied Behavioral Science
Journal of Applied Rehabilitation Counseling
Journal of Autism and Childhood Schizophrenia
Journal of College Student Personnel
Journal of Cross-Cultural Psychology

Journal of Employment Counseling
Journal of the Experimental Analysis of Behavior
Journal of Experimental Child Psychology
Journal of Experimental Social Psychology
Journal of Homosexuality
Journal of Humanistic Psychology
Journal of Individual Psychology
Journal of Marriage and the Family
Journal of Mathematical Psychology
Journal of Motor Behavior
Journal of Non-White Concerns in Personnel and Guidance
Journal of Personality
Journal of Research in Personality
Journal of School Psychology
Journal of the Student Personnel Association for Teacher Education
Journal of Verbal Learning and Verbal Behavior

Learning and Motivation
Life-Threatening Behavior

Measurement and Evaluation in Guidance
Memory & Cognition
Mental Retardation
Monographs of the Society for Research in Child Development
Multivariate Behavioral Research

The Ontario Psychologist
Organizational Behavior and Human Performance

Perception & Psychophysics
Perceptual and Motor Skills
Personnel and Guidance Journal
Personnel Psychology
Physiological Psychology
The Psychological Record
Psychological Reports
Psychology
Psychometrika
Psychophysiology

Rehabilitation Counseling Bulletin
Representative Research in Social Psychology
Review of Educational Research

The School Counselor

Training School Bulletin

The Vocational Guidance Quarterly

Appendix C: Examples of Reference Citations in APA Journals

Kind of Reference	Typewritten Example	Comment
PERIODICALS		
1. Journal article One author	Harlow, H. F. Fundamental principles for preparing psychology journal articles. Journal of Comparative and Physiological Psychology, 1962, 55, 893-896.	
2. Journal article Two authors Journal paginated by issue	Atkinson, R. C., & Shiffrin, R. M. The control of short-term memory. Scientific American, 1971, 225(2), 82-90.	a. If each issue of a journal starts with page 1, include the issue number after the volume number in parentheses.
3. Journal article Corporate author	The Royal Society Conference of Editors. Metrication in scientific journals. American Scientist, 1968, 56, 159-164.	a. Alphabetize corporate authors according to the first significant word of the name (in this case, "Royal").
4. Magazine article Discontinuous pages	Miller, G. A. On turning psychology over to the unwashed. Psychology Today, December 1969, pp. 53-54; 66-74.	a. Even though magazines carry volume numbers, identify them by issue date. b. If an article begins in the front and continues elsewhere, give all page numbers and indicate the discontinuity with a semicolon. c. When the volume number is not given, use "p." or "pp." before the page numbers. When volume and page numbers are both given, omit "Vol." and "p." (see Examples 1–3).

5. Magazine article
   No author

The blood business. <u>Time</u>, September 11, 1972, pp. 47-48.

a. See comments 4a and 4c.
b. If there is no author, begin the entry with the title of the work and alphabetize according to the first significant word of the title (in this case, "blood").
c. In text, the parenthetical citation is: ("The Blood Business," 1972).

6. Newspaper article
   No author
   Discontinuous
   pages

Eight APA journals initiate controversial blind reviewing. <u>APA Monitor</u>, June 1972, pp. 1; 5.

a. See comments 4a–c and 5b.
b. In text, the parenthetical citation is: ("Eight APA Journals," 1972).

7. Monograph with
   issue number
   and serial
   number
   Two authors
   Subtitle

Maccoby, E. E., & Konrad, K. W. The effect of preparatory set on selective listening: Developmental trends. <u>Monographs of the Society for Research in Child Development</u>, 1967, <u>32</u>(4, Serial No. 112).

a. Capitalize the first word of a subtitle.
b. For monographs, give both the issue number and serial (or whole) number to facilitate retrieval.

8. APA monograph
   with whole
   number

Rotter, J. B. Generalized expectancies for internal versus external control of reinforcement. <u>Psychological Monographs</u>, 1966, <u>80</u>(1, Whole No. 609).

a. Examples 8–10 illustrate different ways monographs have been published in APA journals. Each citation is appropriate for a different kind of monograph publication.
b. *Psychological Monographs* were published through 1966.

Kind of Reference	Typewritten Example	Comment

Kind of Reference	Typewritten Example	Comment
9. APA monograph bound separately as a supplement to journal Three authors	Paivio, A., Yuille, J. C., & Madigan, S. A. Concreteness, imagery, and meaningfulness values for 925 nouns. <u>Journal of Experimental Psychology Monograph</u>, 1968, <u>76</u>(1, Pt. 2).	a. See comment 8a. b. Monographs were published as supplements from 1967 to 1970.
10. APA monograph bound into journal with continuous pagination Three authors	Wagner, A. R., Rudy, J. W., & Whitlow, J. W. Rehearsal in animal conditioning. <u>Journal of Experimental Psychology</u>, 1973, <u>97</u>, 407-426. (Monograph)	a. See comment 8a. b. Monographs have been bound into the journals since 1971.
11. Summary in APA Proceedings Proper name in article title	Smart, K. L., & Bruning, J. L. An examination of the practical import of the von Restorff effect. <u>Proceedings of the 81st Annual Convention of the American Psychological Association</u>, 1973, <u>8</u>, 623-624. (Summary)	a. Treat annual books, such as the *Proceedings* and the *Annual Review of Psychology,* as periodicals. However, treat the following exceptions as books: (1) *Nebraska Symposium* (see Example 24) (2) 1965 *Proceedings* because 1966 was Vol. 1 of the *Proceedings.* b. Capitalize a proper name (Restorff) in an article title.
12. Abstract appearing without supporting article	Carpenter, G. C., & Stechler, G. Selective attention to mother's face from Week 1 through Week 8. <u>American Psychologist</u>, 1967, <u>22</u>, 510. (Abstract)	a. If only an abstract is used in research, this citation is appropriate.

13. Citation from a
    secondary source
    Title translated
    into English

Stutte, H. [Transcultural child psychiatry.] <u>Acta Paedopsychiatrica</u>, 1972, <u>38</u>(9), 229-231. (<u>Psychological Abstracts</u>, 1973, <u>49</u>, No. 1067.)

a. See also Example 25.
b. In a few cases, pertinent material is available only from a secondary source. Indicate the secondary source in these rare cases.
c. Use brackets to indicate a translation.
d. In text, cite the date of the original publication (in this case, 1972).

14. Article available
    from the APA
    Journal Supple-
    ment Abstract
    Service (JSAS)

Shaefer, C. D., & Millman, H. L. Behavior change in boys during residential treatment. JSAS <u>Catalog of Selected Documents in Psychology</u>, 1973, <u>3</u>, 88. (Ms. No. 421)

a. This citation is used whether the abstract in the *Catalog* or the full document was used as a source. The citation gives the information necessary for retrieval of either form of the paper.

15. Doctoral disserta-
    tion available on
    University Micro-
    films (and thus
    listed in *Disserta-
    tion Abstracts
    International*)

Shepherd, J. C. An evaluation of group and individual models of career counseling (Doctoral dissertation, University of Utah, 1973). <u>Dissertation Abstracts International</u>, 1973, <u>34</u>, 3071A-3072A. (University Microfilms No. 73-29, 395)

a. See Example 31 for unpublished dissertation available only from a library.
b. Beginning with Vol. 27, *Dissertation Abstracts* paginates in two series, A for humanities and B for sciences.
c. Beginning with Vol. 30, the title of *Dissertation Abstracts* is *Dissertation Abstracts International*.
d. This citation is used whether the abstract, microfilm, or library copy was used as a source. The citation gives the information necessary for retrieval of any of the three forms of the dissertation.

Kind of Reference	Typewritten Example	Comment

PERIODICALS—CONTINUED

16. Reference available from the Educational Resources Information Center (ERIC)

Norberg, K. D. <u>Iconic signs and symbols in audio-visual communication</u>. Sacramento, Calif.: Sacramento State College, 1966. (ERIC Document Reproduction Service No. ED 013 371)

a. This example is the sample ERIC document in *Research in Education,* the ERIC abstract journal. The main entry of the reference gives information on the original document: author and title (in italics because it is available in microform) and the relevant facts of the original publication (where and when the document originated). The parenthetical information enables a person to locate the document through ERIC.

17. Computer program abstracted in *Behavioral Science*

Stoloff, P. H. REGFIT: A curvilinear regression program. <u>Behavioral Science</u>, 1971, <u>16</u>, 518. (CPA 419)

BOOKS

18. Book
Two authors
Second edition
Jr. in name

Strunk, W., Jr., & White, E. B. <u>The elements of style</u> (2nd ed.). New York: Macmillan, 1972.

a. If the place of publication is a well-known city, do not give the state.

b. Give the publisher name in as brief a form as is intelligible.

19. Book
Corporate author
Author as publisher
Revised edition

U.S. Government Printing Office. <u>Style manual</u> (Rev. ed.). Washington, D.C.: Author, 1973.

a. See comment 3a on corporate author.

20. Book
No author

Mathematics in type.
Richmond, Va.: Byrd
Press, 1954.

a. See comment 5b on no author.
b. Place of publication: If several cities have the same name or if the city is obscure, give the state name in abbreviated form.
c. In text, the citation is: (*Mathematics in Type*, 1954).

21. Book in press
Two authors

Hewett, F. M., & Forness,
S. R. Education of
exceptional learners.
Boston: Allyn & Bacon,
in press.

a. In text, the citation is: (Hewett & Forness, in press).
b. Do not give a date until the book is published.

22. All volumes of multivolume, edited work

Maher, B. A. (Ed.). Progress
in experimental personality
research (6 vols.). New
York: Academic Press,
1964-1972.

a. In text, the citation is: (Maher, 1964–1972).

23. Article in an edited book
Two editors
One volume of multivolume work

Riesen, A. H. Sensory depri-
vation. In E. Stellar &
J. M. Sprague (Eds.),
Progress in physiological
psychology (Vol. 1). New
York: Academic Press,
1966.

a. When editors' names are not in author position, do not invert names and do not use a comma between two names.
b. Give page numbers, if needed, with the text citation, not in the reference list.

Kind of Reference	Typewritten Example	Comment

BOOKS—CONTINUED

Kind of Reference	Typewritten Example	Comment
24. Nebraska Symposium Volume in a series	Aronson, E. Some antecedents of interpersonal attraction. In W. J. Arnold & D. Levine (Eds.), Nebraska Symposium on Motivation (Vol. 17). Lincoln: University of Nebraska Press, 1969.	a. Treat the Nebraska Symposium as an edited book. Capitalize the title of the book because it is an official title. b. Place of publication: Do not give the state name because it is part of the publisher's name.
25. Citation from a secondary source	Lindquist, E. F. Design and analysis of experiments in psychology and education. Boston: Houghton Mifflin, 1953.	a. See also Example 13. b. In text, the citation is: Norton (cited in Lindquist, 1953). This citation is used because Lindquist summarizes the results of an unpublished study by Norton. Thus, the Norton reference is most available in a secondary source, the Lindquist book.
26. Article translated within an edited book Volume (roman) part of title of book Reprint from other source	Donders, F. C. [On the speed of mental processes.] In W. G. Koster (Ed. and trans.), Attention and performance II. Amsterdam: North-Holland, 1969. (Reprinted from Acta Psychologica, 1969, 30.)	a. See comment 13c on use of brackets. b. Because the roman numeral is part of the title, do not change it to an arabic numeral. c. The first three volumes of this series are reprints of *Acta Psychologica* volumes.
27. Translated book Edited book A modern reprint of an older edition Republished work	Freud, S. [New introductory lectures in psychoanalysis] (J. Strachey, Ed. and trans.). New York: Norton, 1965. (Originally published, 1933.)	a. In text, the citation is: (Freud, 1933/1965). Give both dates to place the work chronologically in text and to locate the entry in the reference list.

28. Technical report available from the National Technical Information Service (NTIS)

Gordon, M. A., & Bottenberg, R. A. _Prediction of unfavorable discharge by separate educational levels_ (PRL-TRD-62-5). Lackland Air Force Base, Tex.: 6570th Personnel Research Laboratory, Aerospace Medical Division, April 1962. (NTIS No. AD-284 802)

a. If the report is _not_ available from NTIS or the Government Printing Office, cite it as a reference _note_, not in the reference list (see section 3.61).

29. Government publication available from the Government Printing Office (GPO)

Clements, S. D. _Minimal brain dysfunction in children_ (NINDS Monograph No. 3, U.S. Public Health Service Publication No. 1415). Washington, D.C.: U.S. Government Printing Office, 1966.

a. See comment 28a.

30. Human Resources Research Organization (HumRRO) technical report

Miller, E. E. _A taxonomy of response processes_ (HumRRO Tech. Rep. 69-16). Alexandria, Va.: Human Resources Research Organization, September 1969.

a. HumRRO reports are widely available. They frequently have ERIC and NTIS numbers as well (see Examples 16 and 28).

31. Unpublished doctoral dissertation available from library

Lightburn, L. T. _The relation of critical fusion frequency to age_. Unpublished doctoral dissertation, University of New Jersey, 1951.

a. If dissertation is available on microfilm, use Example 15.

129

Kind of Reference	Typewritten Example	Comment

MISCELLANEOUS CITATIONS—CONTINUED

32. Film

Wolff, L. (Producer). <u>Rock-</u>
<u>a-bye baby</u>. New York:
Time-Life Films, 1971.
(Film)

a. See Example 33 for citation of a review of this film.

33. Review of a film or book

Dokecki, P. R. When the
bough breaks . . . What
will happen to baby?
(Review of <u>Rock-a-bye baby</u>
by L. Wolff). <u>Contemporary</u>
<u>Psychology</u>, 1973, <u>18</u>, 64.

a. If the review does not have a title of its own, take the parenthetical material out of parentheses and move it to the title position of the entry.
b. See Example 32 for citation of this film.

Index

Decimal numbers in roman type refer to sections of the Publication Manual. **Numbers in boldface refer to pages of the Manual.**

TABLES

FIGURES